FORBIDDEN

FRUIT

Copyright © 2008 by Simone

ISBN 978-0-6152-0614-1

Preface

We are all familiar with the phrase 'Easier said than done' and there are times in our lives we find ourselves in a situation where a decision has to be made. What do you do when the choice you're faced with lies between following your heart and doing what your mind tells you is right?

As you read the stories in this book, entertain the idea of what you would do in each of the scenarios these characters found themselves faced with. Would you have the will power to walk away? Or would you fall victim to your own emotional and physical desires as well?

Table of Contents

Your Meal, My Ticket

What kind of friend am I? I recently found myself flirting with my best friend's boyfriend. Shit. What am I going to do? Today Mimi called me on the phone to complain about her boy friend, Trey. That's all she does, complain about him. She keeps talking about how clingy he is and about how she thinks he's all sprung. The other day she asked me to meet him at the bowling alley for her so she could go to some party.

I've known Trey since the 5ᵗʰ grade and I met Mimi in the 9ᵗʰ grade. At first, Trey and I had a really cool and laid back type of friendship going on. We never really flirted with each other, but some of our mutual friends used to joke about how much time we spent together and about how they just knew we were doing more than just *hanging out. To be honest with you, I didn't really consider him my type and I was even more sure that he didn't look at me that way. Mimi came to our school in the 9th grade and like all new girls, the guys were all over her but she was the type of chick that dated a guy based on his stats. She found out I was friends with Trey, who was the captain of the football team and she asked me to hook them up. He was a shy guy trapped in a jocks body and world. He wasn't like the other guys in our school who played sports. He wasn't all self centered like they were.*

So anyway, they started dating at the end of 9th grade and have been off and on ever since. Here we are about to graduate in a few weeks and they're still going. I was there for both of them every time they broke up and got back together. She'd dump him, so she could be with other guys and be free of guilt. Of course she would blame it on *some bullshit reason or other. He'd always take her back after she played the crying game.*

I dated other guys but found myself alone in my room on the phone with Trey most nights. Usually Mimi had stood him up and I recently dumped another guy for being a jerk. Our conversations usually started with things like, "Damn Trey, I don't know how you deal with all her shit. You must really love her...I wish I could find a guy like that." Then he would say something like, "You are too good for the assholes you date." And our conversations ended with things like, "If I were your man, you wouldn't want for anything. I would treat you like the princess you are." And I would say something like, "If I was your girl you'd never need to find comfort elsewhere. You would be treated like the great guy you truly are."

So tonight I went out with; Trey, Mimi, and Jason who was my flavor of the month. First we all caught a movie. Jason was on my right, Trey was on my left and Mimi was on his other side. Mimi was leaning away from Trey talking on her cell and Jason fell asleep in the first 25 minutes of the movie. Trey and I found ourselves making jokes about the old couple who sat in front of us. There was a moment where we both reach for the soda and our fingers ran over each other. We made eye contact and I could feel his eyes penetrate my soul. We seemed to be in a world of own. Our dates were uninterested and we were left to entertain each other. So many things crossed my mind in that instance. I could kiss him and feel what I've been longing to feel again for so long. I could smell popcorn on his breath and his lips were glazed with butter. Popcorn never smelled so good to me before. I wanted to feel his lips against mine, but then I regained my composure. What if Jason woke up or Mimi suddenly got off the phone. We would be found out. No, we couldn't let that happen. So, we looked away and suppressed our desires once more.

It all started at a party about a year ago. Mimi begged me to go with her and Jason but I didn't want to feel like a third wheel because I was in between flavors at the time, but she nagged and nagged so I went. About midnight some fools got the idea that we should all play truth or dare, of course, Mimi wouldn't let me sit that out. One of Trey's teammates who used to make jokes about us being more than friends dared him to kiss me. Trey tried to back out by saying he had a girlfriend but Mimi's crazy ass was like, "No, go ahead. I don't care if you do it. It's not a big deal." Then she had the nerve to say, "Make sure you throw some tongue in there for good measure." I thought she was out of her freaking mind, but I guess she was just tipsy. Everyone was waiting and staring intensely at us. I said, "Screw it, let's just get it over with so they'll quit gawking." But as we began to lean in towards each other we made eye contact and something in my stomach began to tighten. The closer he got to me the faster my heart began to beat.

I thought that everyone could see my heart about to pound out of my chest. As he got closer and closer I could smell the margarita on his breath. Our lips met and I felt my body melt. Some one in the background reiterated Mimi's tongue comment and I felt his tongue slide between my lips and for whatever reason I couldn't and didn't want to fight the tingling feeling that began to flow through my body.

Our tongues began to play and it felt like there was no one else in the room but us. I didn't want to stop and he didn't seem like he was going to pull away any time soon. I was brought back to reality when someone said, "Damn, they're really getting into it, aren't they?" We pulled away and our eyes remained locked until we sat back down and Mimi tugged at his arm complaining about how she was ready to go.

After that we avoided being alone together and our late night conversations ceased for about one month. We avoided eye contact as much as possible because every time we made eye contact it seemed we both remembered that night at the party. We never discussed the kiss and we went back to our late night conversations one night when I called Mimi and she told me she was getting ready for a night on the town, so I should call Trey if I needed a shoulder to lean on. I did, so I called and cried to him over the phone about how I had met a guy that I thought was really going to be good to me this time but I found out he had had a girlfriend for the past 3 years. I was the other woman.

Trey just listened and tried to comfort me as best he could. He told me that if I wanted him to come over to keep me company he would, and so he did. We sat on my front steps for about 4 hours. I mostly cried on his shoulder at first, then he would say something to make me laugh and by the time he left, I had forgotten all about my newly broken heart.

I had been asleep for a while when Trey called. It was late, but he was always there for me and he knew he could call me whenever he needed to talk and I knew something had to be up with him, because he rarely called this late.

"Hello."

"Hey, its me," he said as if I didn't know his sensual voice by now, *"I'm sorry to call you this late but I just couldn't sleep and I really didn't want to talk to Mimi right now and I couldn't think of any one else, but you."*

"What's wrong, Trey? It's ok, just talk to me sweetie." Damn, did I just call him sweetie, did he hear that? Shit, I'm tired. I hope he didn't hear that.

"Well, it's about Mimi." When has it ever not been about Mimi trampling all over his feelings? *"I don't think I can deal with her anymore. I really don't. I mean, I think she's just using me to get out of this town, you know?"*

Hell yeah, I knew that, but I didn't want to just come out and say that shit before, but maybe it's time he heard the ugly truth. I didn't know how he was going to

*take it but I had to just come out with it.
"Well, it's about time you realize that shit.
She's been using you ever since she found
out there were scouts checking you out." He
probably didn't expect me to come at him
like that but shit, it was time we got real.
Maybe I'm just tired, I don't know. He
didn't quite seem to know what to say, so I
continued.*

*"I mean damn Trey; she's been
shitting on you for a long time now. You
need to stop letting her take advantage of
you and go find another freaking meal
ticket."*

*"Damn, how long have you been
feeling this way and why haven't you said
anything."*

*"Well, I didn't want to get all up in
your business and I damn sure didn't want
to seem like I was trying to hate on you or*

her, you know what I mean?" Then he came out of left field with his next question.

"Can you come over right now?"

"What?! Do you know what time it is?"

"I have something I want to tell you, but I need to tell you in person."

"Why? Why can't you just tell me over the phone? What it is?" I was totally confused. His question was just too random.

"I need to look into your eyes when I say what I need to say because I need to see your reaction. I can't tell you over the phone."

"Well, can't it wait till the sun comes up at least?" What could be so damn important, I thought to myself.

"By then I might not have the courage to say it...please just come over."

"Shit." I didn't really want to have to get dressed, make sure I looked decent and

smelled good. I figured if it was so important then he should be willing to come over to my place, plus my parents were out of town.

"How about you just come over here, how about that?"

"I know how your parents are, you're father will probably try to shoot my ass. No way!"

I had to laugh at that one. "They're not here, just come over, but make it quick, ok."

"Ok, see you in a bit." Before I could say another word he hung up. He lived ten minutes from me but it seemed like not even five minutes had passed before I heard a gentle tap on my window. I went down to let him in and before I could get the door open completely, he slid inside and kissed me. He kissed me deeply and intensely. I felt my temperature go up about 15 degrees. He pressed me up against the door and grabbed

my face and kissed me like kissing me could save his life. I was still in shock after he finally managed to pull himself away. I sat on the stairs wondering if I was dreaming and if maybe I fell asleep on the phone or maybe the call was part of the dream too, but it wasn't a dream. I pinched myself to make sure... I was without words.

He stood there looking at me for a while before sitting next to me. Then he finally decided to speak.

"Well, that's what I wanted to tell you. I didn't quite know how to tell you that over the phone and I know that if I waited till I saw you after class, I wouldn't have the balls the do it."

I didn't really know how to respond to that. I just sat looking back at him. He began to look discouraged and I kissed him again, just as deeply and intensely as he had kissed me and then the words came to me.

"Well, that was my response to what you had to tell me." We both smiled and kissed again. It felt so good to let out all the tension that had been bottled up inside of us for so long.

We made love that night like we were two long lost souls who had finally been reunited. He broke up with Mimi for good the following day and we ended up going to prom together. My excuse to Mimi was that I felt sorry for him since she had already had a date lined up to go with even before they broke up. Prom night was like a dream come true. I never in a million years imagined that I would have been with Trey. He treated me like I was the most beautiful girl there and we barely saw Mimi and her date that night.

Trey got drafted to the NFL and plays for the Eagles and it just so happened that I got accepted to a university in Philadelphia.

I didn't think he would still be interested in me after he got into the pros, but he proposed to me junior year and we got married right after I graduated. We are still in love and we still have late night phone calls from time to time. As far as Mimi goes, I heard she moved to Vegas and started stripping. I also heard she found herself a rich doctor who was willing to spend all his money on her. I guess she still got her meal ticket.

The # 2 From Brooklyn

*Damn, I need to get home. I've had a
long ass day, but if I could just get on the
Subway and get to bed I would be fine, but
I'm sure that with the way these people are
moving I'll miss my train, which means I
won't see that sexy ass guy that gets on
there everyday around this time. I think he's
usually coming from work. Sometimes he
has his dreads up in a fashionable,
sophisticated bun. That's usually when I see
him wearing a classy business suit. He looks
so sexy in those navy blue, heather gray, and
chocolate colored suits, it drives me crazy.
Sometimes he just has his hair pulled back
in a ponytail. That's when I see him wearing
his 'play' clothes, or so I like to call them.
He's not quite hip-hop, but he's not*

*American Eagle either. He's more in
between. I love the way he can just have on
a pair of jeans and a Bob Marley t-shirt and
drive me insane. I've been noticing this guy
for about a month now. I almost feel like I'm
dating him, but we've never spoken, not
even a simple hello. Maybe that one day
when he said hi to me as I was getting off
and he was getting on. Yea, I remember that.
I damn near had an orgasm that day. Oh my
god. I can just imagine what it would be like
making love to him. Man, fuck that, I don't
want to make love. I want him to bang my
back out. Straight fuck the shit out of me.
Damn, I can't believe I'm talking like this, I
don't even know this guy. I don't usually say
things like that but this guy has some
strange type of sex appeal. The type of man
that just makes you want to fuck. It's crazy, I
know.*

Teaching night school wasn't the best idea I've ever had. I don't know what the hell I was thinking. Those damn people get to me. I started this night school teaching thing about a month and a half ago, and ever since then even though I don't really like it, I look forward to seeing my mystery man every night on the number 2 from Brooklyn. His skin is like baked banana nut bread, so golden brown and smooth. His eyes are like delicious brownies, dark and sexy. His lips, damn those lips. They're always moist and they look so full and soft. I hope I see him tonight. It would make my whole weekend better. Especially since I don't have any dates lined up and no man to go home to, just seeing him would make it all better.

I finally get through the mass crowd of people standing around like they have nowhere to go. I mean shit, it's Friday night and it's almost 11:30...shouldn't they be headed to the clubs or where ever they go? Damn, I think I see him up ahead...he's wearing his work clothes. A dark blue suit, with a royal blue shirt and tie to match. Boy did he know how to look sexy for me.

I pushed my way through the crowd as the number 2 pulled up. I knew he'd be getting on. I jumped on and waited for the doors to close, then made my way through the cars until I saw him standing at the far end of one. Damn, there he is looking so tired from a long day at work. Looking so fucking sexy. Maybe tonight I will say something. I made my way closer. Shit, I'm getting wet thinking about the possibilities. The train stopped and more people got on pushing me closer to him. I was so close to him I could feel his breath on my cheek. It smelled like strawberries. And his cologne was so subtle and mesmerizing; so sexy. As the train shook and rattled, our bodies rubbed up against each other. I thought to myself, say something, say something. He's right in front of you! But nothing came out. When the train stopped again, I felt so bad I decided to go to a different car, but as people came and went I just got pinned where I was.

This time I was faced the other way. I felt somewhat embarrassed and disappointed in myself. I've got to quit being so timid. The train shook and rattled some more. The lights went out and the train sounded like it was going to stop. As it came to a screeching halt, the force of the other passengers pushed my body up against his, but I wasn't complaining.

When the train stopped, I didn't move. And neither did he. I felt myself getting wetter and wetter. I grabbed the poll and tried not to think dirty thoughts but I couldn't help it. I felt something on my ass; I know it was his dick because there was no way he could have gotten his hands in-between us. Shit, when opportunity knocks I hear you're supposed to open the door. This was my chance to open the door. So I leaned into it. I felt him squeeze through other passengers and put a hand on my waist and I leaned even harder. I felt his dick get harder and I liked it. He leaned into me and I thought he was about to say speak, but instead he kissed me gently behind my left ear. I started moving my hips on his dick, which was growing by the minute. That shit made me wet for sure. His hand moved hesitantly upward towards my breasts. He caressed them and played with my nipples. He must have put down his briefcase because I felt his other hand pulling up my skirt.

I'm thinking oh shit, he's about to find out how horny I am for him, but fuck it, I want him to know. I want him, period. His hand reached my pussy, and he played with their lips. Damn, it was about to start 'raining'. He used his other hand to grab my neck and arch it backward. Our lips met and we kissed passionately, and long. I reached behind me and grabbed his dick with my right hand and with my left I grabbed the back of his head and pressed him even further into me. Suddenly he stopped. I couldn't see him really, only the small flicker of light that shone in his eyes. He spun me around and our eyes locked. I was too overwhelmed to speak and I think he was too. We kissed again. Our hands were all over each other. By this time he had turned me around and pussy was pressed up against his dick and I wanted to fuck right then and there. I started to unbuckle his belt and he pulled my skirt up even more. This time he played with my pussy so vigorously and gently at the same time, I came. I pulled out his dick and started stroking it. I stroked it until he came, and to my surprise he was still hard.

I loved this man whose name I didn't even know. He put his hand up to his face and licked his fingers, I did the same. I guided his dick into my pussy and was impressed at how much he was working with. I hadn't realized just how big his dick was. I gasped for air and he became aware that he had a little more than I was used to handling, so he gently glided inside me while raising my right leg up and around his waist.

This is finally the point when I realized there were other people around because as he lifted my leg it brushed against a man standing next to him, but it was too late to turn back now and frankly I didn't give a fuck. I wanted this man, whatever his name was. I decided to go with the flow and I put all of myself on that dick. We were grinding and kissing and touching simultaneously and it felt good. My body was about to explode. I could feel him tense up as if he was about to cum. He pressed me up against the poll and I grabbed his hair as he grabbed mine. His tongue was basically fucking mine and damn, did it make me cream. We moved a little more vigorously and grinded like we were trying to break each others hips without making a sound. I couldn't moan…I just exhaled. His muscles tensed and so did mine. I saw him closed his eyes as he pushed deeper inside me, making me close mine. Then, we both climaxed.

The train started moving again, but the lights didn't come back on. We kissed and parted, fixing our clothes. When the lights came back on the conductor told us we would have to get off and switch trains. I tried to think of something to say. He seemed to be doing the same.

We got off the train and onto the platform. We stood next to each other, not saying a word. We acted like total strangers, which is exactly what we were. The next train came and we both got on. No words. The lights went out again. He grabbed me and kissed me like it was the last kiss he would ever have on earth and I responded the same way. We parted again.

The train stopped in Penn Station. We both got off and went our separate ways. I turned around and looked at him one last time. We made eye contact and said goodbye with our eyes. Then, he walked away and I did the same. I never saw him again.

Family Affairs Of The Heart

"Nancy, you can send in Mr. Edwards now," Debra said as she released the button on the telephone and leaned back into leather high back chair. Debra Worthington was the president of a very popular magazine in New York City. Her once exciting career has now become nothing more than connecting flights and pseudo cordiality with other business execs.

"Hey Deb, how's it going?" Jacob Edwards asks. He was the CEO of the accounting firm that handles the magazines profits. They were long time friends and colleagues. He'd always thought Debra was a great catch and didn't understand how a woman of such education, success, not to mention good looks, was not married. She

stood only five foot five, but you would never know it because Debra wore high heels, at least three and half inches tall, everywhere she went. She had long hair which was always in a conservative ponytail or bun and underneath her business suits was a woman with great curves.

"I'm doing well, Jake. How is the family?" She noticed Jake fiddling with his wedding band, something he did only if he was worried or uneasy about asking for a favor.

"What is it Jake, you've never been good at hiding things from me so just spit it out." Jake was only slightly older than Debra at forty-nine but looked almost sixty. She remember the days when female associates would huddle in corners and chatter about how sexy Jake was, but became silent as soon as she walked by. Jake wasn't very tall, only about five foot

eight, but he carried himself as if he thought he was taller. He had penetrating brown eyes and a smile that could con a salesman.

"Alright Deb, here's the deal. My son Anthony is in a little bind and unfortunately good 'old Daddy can't help him this time."

"Little Tony?" Debra remembered seeing him some years ago at a family dinner.

"Well, 'little Tony' got himself kicked out of school and needs a job. And to think he was working on his second degree, a more serious one than first. Can you believe he had the nerve to get a degree in performing arts?" He said sarcastically. "I was so happy he had finally come to his senses and was perusing a business degree. Anyway, he's back in the area, but it seems like no one is looking to hire. He's good with numbers, but my company is not

interested in letting go their best in order to make room for 'little Tony'.

Debra was beginning to get what Jake was asking for. "I'll see if my finance department is in need of any assistance, but I can't promise you anything and he can't expect to just hop into a top salary position. He's going to have to start at the bottom."

"Good enough for me. I don't care what he does; he just has to do it fast. Kathy and I were just getting used to having the house all to ourselves, especially since Pete just went off to college this past fall." Jake stared off into the ceiling imagining the things he and Kathy were now able to do with the boys out of the house.

Two weeks passed and Debra hadn't heard from Jake or 'little Tony'. She began to think that maybe things worked out for him and he no longer needed a job. Just then she received a page on her intercom from her secretary.

"Mrs. D, there's an Anthony Edwards here to see you."

"Ok Nancy, have him wait ten minutes then send him in." Debra always made visitors; especially potential employees wait, just to give them time to either relax or work up into a nervous mess. The ones who relaxed usually got a second interview.

As Anthony entered the room, Debra looked up from her desk and was almost shocked to see that 'little Tony' had now grown into a very attractive young man, at 25 with he had a striking resemblance to his father. He was now 6'1"and 185lbs of lean muscles. He was surprised as well, to see that Mrs. D, whom he'd always thought was very attractive, seemed even more so, sitting in her office with her business attire on. It seemed as if she hadn't aged at all since he's last saw her. She looked intimidating, but seductive at the same time.

Debra got up from her desk and walked toward him and embraced him. "Hi Tony, it's good to see you. How have you been?"

"I've been better, but I'm ok. I want to thank you for giving me an opportunity. I really appreciate it and so does my father."

"Well, I want you to understand something Tony…" Before she could continue he interjected.

"I would prefer if you call me Anthony, I feel it is a bit more professional in the work place."

"Ok Anthony, in that case you can call me Mrs. Worthington and do not interrupt me when I'm speaking."

The interview continued and ended in a professional, almost cold tone. Somehow, his interjection, also injected a chill into the atmosphere.

"I look forward to seeing you bright and early Monday morning at 8 a.m. sharp."

"8 a.m.?" Tony wasn't used to having to arrive at work until at least 10 a.m.

"Is that a problem for you, Mr. Edwards?" Her tone was stern and unwavering.

"No, not at all Mrs. Worthington." He knew that he needed this job in order to move into his own place and as much as his parents didn't want him back home, he didn't want to be there either. He missed the freedom he had to come and go as he pleased and do what he pleased, when he

pleased. He felt like a child again and it wasn't sitting well with him.

Debra went home to her Park Avenue home that Friday evening with Chinese food in one hand and two videos from Blockbuster in the other. Lately she had become quite the movie buff, since her love life has been on a hiatus.

Debra had recently parted ways with her most recent love interest, Michael Owens an investment banker who was ready to settle down. The idea of settling down is not what caused the split, but more so his desire to move to Washington D.C. He had gotten an offer that he couldn't refuse and asked Debra to relocate with him. She said yes then had a change of heart, but didn't tell him until they were at the airport getting ready to board a flight. That was eight months ago.

She still thinks about what life would have been like living with Michael, but believes it would not have been the life that would fill the void she had been feeling for so long. She didn't want or need the monotonous, day to day life of two married business people whose only real conversations were rooted in the weather, traffic and the stock market. She wanted to feel alive; she wanted Broadway shows, Jazz concerts, trips to Venice and spontaneous romantic rendezvous'.

Saturday night one of Debra's friends called inquiring about whether or not Debra wanted to attend a poetry contest. Debra couldn't quite say no, being that she was an avid reader of poetry. She met up with her girlfriends: Sharon, a real estate attorney who looked more like a spice girl and thought she was twenty five. Nicole, an HR director for a top financial company who could not keep her legs closed if she tried, and tried she did. Then there was Christine, an advertising agent who was the most stable of the three.

When she arrived at the location, the crowd looked well mixed. There were twenty-something's, thirty-something's, forty-something's and even a few fifty-something peppered through out the crowd. Some wore their office attire, others wore urban gear, and some wore more retro clothing. As she entered the foyer, she saw her girlfriends at the bar ordering drinks, she assumed they were ready to party because they usually didn't start drinking until after the artists started reciting their poetry.

"Hello, ladies." Debra greeted her girlfriends with hugs and friendly kisses on the cheek.

"Hey Deb, how have you been? Seems like since Michael left town, you have been hard to get a hold of, are you still longing for him?" Sharon asked, with a slight grin knowing that Debra didn't like when she referred to Michael as if he left her.

"You know that I left him and not the other way around." Debra responded with a slightly annoyed tone. Then Christine chimed in, "These two were sitting here betting on whether or not you would make a comment or simply ignore the reference to Michael." She giggled.

As the night went on, Sharon and Nicole began getting louder and more obnoxious while Christine and Debra slowly sipped their drinks and chatted about their careers and love lives. Just as Nicole finished describing her recent sexual disappointment with her boy toy of the month, a waitress brought over a round of drinks.

"Hi, a young man asked me to bring these over to you ladies and wanted me to tell you he can't wait to see you," the waitress said to Debra as she pointed to the other side of the room, where a group young people were sitting around a table in a corner. Debra couldn't quite make out anyone's face, as the club was dark and smoky.

Debra's girlfriends made a joke about the anonymous drinks only for a few moments, and then went back to their stories.

As they started to make their way towards the exit, a young man gently touched Debra on her elbow and to her surprise when she turned around, she saw

Tony standing there with a very drunk looking woman barely hanging onto his arm.

"Mrs. Worthington, I didn't think you came to places like this." Tony looked as if he had had a few drinks himself.

Debra was slightly uncomfortable seeing her employees outside of the office. She hated feeling like she was being judged or criticized by them.

"I could say the same thing of you, Mr. Edwards." She was desperately trying to keep a professional tone between them as she knew her girlfriends were watching very closely.

"I guess that means we have more in common than just work, huh?" Tony said this with a flirtatious smile that quickly vanished when he saw Debra's disdain.

"I wouldn't go that far," Debra said as she turned and continued outside but not

before she said, "8 a.m. sharp," over her right shoulder.

"Nancy, what does my schedule look like today?" Debra asked through the intercom.

"Not much, Mrs. D. You have a short day; you have a conference call at eleven and nothing before that."

"Great, that means I can go home early today and if everything is good, then you can go home early as well, ok Nancy?"

"Sounds good, Mrs. D."

Debra was sitting in her office watching the morning news when Nancy came through the speaker. "Mrs. D, there's a Mr. Edwards here to see you." She didn't recall Jake saying he'd be stopping by, but if he did stop by this early there must be something he needed to talk about.

"Ok, show him in." Debra put the T.V. on mute and waited, she wanted Jake to know that he had her undivided attention and that she was there for him but to her surprise Jake is not who walked through the door. She quickly turned the T.V. off not wanting to seem the least bit unprofessional.

Tony noticed her fidgeting and asked in a sly tone of voice, "Did you forget I was coming?"

Debra glanced over at the clock and saw that it was 7:55 a.m. he was early. "I didn't forget, just didn't think you would show up until maybe noon. Isn't that the norm for you college boys?"

Tony wasn't fond of what she was trying to imply and quickly readjusted his posture and tone of voice to something more professional. He was intent on being taken seriously. Yes, she was a friend of his dad but she was now also his boss.

They spoke for another 15 minutes about what she expected from him, what his duties were and that he would not be given any special treatment. As the conversation ended, they shook hands and Debra showed him to the door. He informed her of how much he appreciated the opportunity and assured her that she would not regret giving him a chance.

The rest of Debra's day went quite smoothly and she was able to leave the office at 1p.m., an early Monday is always a good thing Debra thought to herself. In the elevator on the way down to the lobby she received a phone call from Jake but the reception was bad and she told him she would call him when she got out of the building. She forgot all about calling Jake when a man in the parking lot almost ran her over. As she drove home, all she could think about was how it might not have been such a bad idea if she'd gone with Michael to D.C.

When she entered her apartment she instantly felt lonely and depressed. There was no one there to welcome her home, no one to hug or kiss, and no one to talk to. She decided a long, hot bath would be just the thing she needed. As she lay in the tub trying to relax, she heard her cell going off in the bedroom. Jake! She'd forgotten all about him.

When she got out of the bath and checked her phone, there were three new messages waiting. The first said, "Hey Deb, it's me. Call me when you get a quick minute." The second said, "Deb, it's me again. Sorry to keep bugging like this. Umm, well...call me when you can." Debra realized that Jake's voice got a little more strained in the second message. The third message said, "Hey, umm...call me. I need to talk to you." Jake now sounded desperate, Debra was beginning to worry. She called him as soon as the final message ended.

"Hello," Jake answered the phone in a low, scratchy voice.

"It's Deb, is everything ok? I'm sorry I didn't get back to you sooner. Are you alright?" The anxiety was clear in her voice.

"Hey Deb, its cool. Can we talk?"

"Definitely, tell me what's wrong?" Debra felt like he was hesitating. "You can talk to me about anything, what's up Jake? You got me worried!"

"I'd rather talk in person; can I come to your office?" Jake was so accustomed to Debra working late; he naturally assumed she was still there.

"I'm not at the office, I'm at home. If you're in the neighborhood, you can swing by or I can meet you somewhere." Debra was getting antsy.

Jake showed up at Debra's house thirty minutes after they had gotten off the phone. When he arrived he looked tired, beaten down and he reeked of alcohol. Debra was now really concerned. She had never seen Jake like this. She had seen him angry, hurt and even drunk and sad, but never like this.

"Jake, you're scaring me. What's going on?" Debra was speaking in a stern yet caring tone. She didn't like seeing her good friend looking like this. He took his arms from around her, walked over to her couch and sat down without saying a word. His posture was slouched; his eyes bloodshot and he looked like he hadn't

shaved in days. This wasn't the well groomed, sophisticated Jake she had always known. She walked over to him, sat down and waited.

"Kathy kicked me out," Jake blurted out as if his lips had betrayed his desire to hold in his comment. He leaned back and placed a hand over his eyes as if to hide the tears.

"What do you mean she kicked you out? Why would she do that? What happened?" Debra had a million questions racing through her heard. She just wanted to get to the bottom of this.

"She said that if I couldn't love her completely, then I don't need to love her at all. She's mad Deb, really mad." He wasn't making any sense. What was he talking about? Debra couldn't put the pieces together.

"Jake, slow down. I don't understand." She wondered if Kathy had found out about the affair he had had years ago when they were on the outs. *"Does she know about what happened with you know who?"*

"She already knew about that," Jake said to Debra's surprise. She wasn't aware that Kathy had known about that all this time. *"She over heard a conversation I was having with a colleague about a woman."*

"You did it again, Jake?" Debra asked hurriedly and with a slightly unsympathetic tone. Debra thought to herself that she would have kicked him out too if she took a man back after he cheated and he had the nerve to do it again.

"No, Deb!" Jake responded with an offended grimace. *"I didn't do it again."* Jake fell silent as if he had changed his mind about talking to her about his problems.

"I'm sorry. Tell me what happened."

"Well, I really can't go into detail or name names but I will tell you that I never had any intentions of betraying her again."

"Ok, so what happened?"

"Mike, the guy who works in marketing, you remember him," Jake asked rhetorically, *"well he called the other day and Kathy answered, when I picked up the phone in the other room I guess she thought she had hung up, but she didn't."* He stopped and looked at Debra as if needing reassurance before continuing. She obliged him.

"Go on Jake, I'm listening."

"Well, to make a long story short, she heard Mike ask me about whether or not I was going to confess my feelings for a particular person Kathy and I both know very well." Debra wasn't sure how to react. She wasn't sure if she should even ask any

*questions, but she still wanted to be
supportive.*

*"Wow, umm...so what are you going
to do? Does this other woman know now?"*

*"No, she doesn't, but I mean what is
there to lose now that Kathy has thrown me
out?" He sounded defeated.*

*They continued to talk but Jake never
revealed to Debra who the other woman
was, only saying that Debra was familiar
with who the woman is and would be
surprised if she found out. They eventually,
got around to talking about other things
before Jake left saying he was headed to a
friend's house. Debra felt sorry for Jake but
somehow felt that karma had worked its'
way back around to Jake for the affair he
had.*

The rest of Debra's week was full of the same old boring things; business meetings, teleconferencing, and presentations. She mad a decision that she would dedicate this weekend to herself. She planned to have an early afternoon on Friday where she could get some spa time. She wanted and needed to be pampered, plus sometimes she was lucky enough to get an attractive male masseuse. Sounds desperate, but when you're not getting any loving a nice rub down from the opposite sex is always great.

Friday could not have arrived soon enough. Debra left her office at 2p.m. on the dot and didn't have any qualms about it. She was out of there. She enjoyed her three hours at the spa. She got a full body wrap, a massage, and a mani-pedi. She went home feeling refreshed, relaxed and calm. She ate dinner in bed alone while watching random

TV shows. She flipped through the channels until she fell asleep. She was awakened by a call from Christine around 10p.m. who had Nicole on three-way who also had Sharon on the other line.

"Hey girl, you coming out with us tonight," Christine asked in an upbeat and slightly tipsy manner.

"No, I don't think so. Maybe next week." Debra was definitely not in the mood for those women tonight. She was in a mellower mood and wanted to try and keep it that way.

Her friends were disappointed but they quickly recovered. They had forgotten all about Debra by the time they all met up at some new club uptown.

Debra decided to take a trip to her favorite jazz cafe, Mystic Groove. It was mellow, not too loud or busy and the crowd was mature. When she arrived, there was a small group of people at the door waiting to get in and a few more people hastily approaching. Was there something special going on tonight, Debra though to herself.

She finally got inside and was seated at a table to the far right of the stage. She got herself comfortable and relaxed as she sat back, sipped on an Amoretto Sour, and listened to the band play their jazzy rendition of Yesterday. As the night went on, one of the ushers noticed that Debra hadn't arrived with anyone and placed three people at the table with her. Debra was feeling too mellow to even be bothered by it. She just kept on tapping her foot to the music and enjoyed herself.

The MC walked onto the stage and announced that a new performer was about to get on a do his thing.

"Alright people, we got something special for you tonight! My main man is about to come on and make you ladies fall in love," he said in a sexy tone and the ladies started whistling and cheering.

"I want ya'll to sit back, relax and let the music move you…And now without further a due, my man, my friend, Mr. Eddie T!!" and the women went crazy again.

Debra didn't understand. Had it been that long since she'd been out, she had never heard of this guy and he must have had talent, the place was packed. She saw a man walk onto the stage with a guitar and a stool. He looked sort of grungy in Debra's opinion. He wore jeans, a Jimi Hendrix T-shirt and a raggedy looking Army jacket. His baseball hat was worn so low, you couldn't see his eyes. Debra wasn't impressed and didn't see what the big deal was.

Eddie T placed the stool in front of the microphone, sat down and with out a word began to sing in a voice that seemed too beautiful to be coming from someone who looked like that.

"I'm not telling you I love you because I'm afraid of what you might say," he sang while he strummed his guitar and the band followed his lead. "Yet I long for you each and every day." His voice had a John Mayer feel but with a hint more soulfulness. You could hear a pin drop as he sang his song that seemed to touch every woman's soul, even Debra's. She hadn't taken another sip of her drink since he started his ballad and almost didn't realize that she had begun to tear up as he sang. She tried hard to look over and around the crowd to get a better glimpse of the man whose words had made her cry from her soul, but couldn't.

As he finished his song singing, "If I let you into my heart will you protect it, would your heart then let me in." He walked off stage the same way he entered, without a word. The women wanted more; they clapped and cheered and whistled. Even the men were applauded. Eddie T, walked back on stage, took a bow and vanished once again, leaving without a word.

When Debra got home that night, all she could think about was this guy she had never heard of; Eddie T. She wondered where he was from, how old he was and if that was even his real name. She fell asleep holding her pillow, wishing it was him.

The next evening she called Mystic Groove and asked if Eddie T would be performing again. The receptionist said he wasn't scheduled to perform but he sometimes came the night after a performance, just to get some feedback from his performance the night before and that on occasion he would hop on stage and do a little something. And on that note, Debra was determined to be in the house and to be center stage.

Earlier in the day she had called Christine and ranted about how good he was and how she thought the girls would love him. They decided to make it a girls' night out and so it was.

They arrived at 9p.m. and there was no line, as a matter of fact it seemed pretty dead and Debra's girlfriends were ready to complain. They were able to get a table close to stage, but Debra was feeling low, knowing he wasn't scheduled to perform and it looked like the chances of him stopping by were slim. Not only did she long to hear his voice again, but she was not in the mood to hear her girlfriends complain about how she had dragged them to some funky jazz café.

The girls were starting to get antsy, so Debra ordered a round in hopes that it would help them mellow out. She was beginning to wish she hadn't invited them in the first place.   The band was playing and Christine and Nicole had decided to go mingle. Just then, the MC got on the microphone. "Hey, I got some good news and some bad news. What do you want first?" The audience yelled out their answers and seemed to be right at home with the MC's interactive approach. "Well, I'm gonna give you the bad news first. As you all know, Eddie T is a big hit here at Mystic and had a wonderful performance last night," The crowd cheers and whistles, "but he is not scheduled to perform tonight." The crowd moaned and booed in unison. "The good news is that ya'll can come back next week and see him do his thing again." He starts to walk away from the mic as the crowd continues to display their displeasure. Then he runs back over to the mic and says, "Just kidding, Eddie T is here and he will be doing one of his most popular songs… Telling you I love you." The crowd, including Debra gets on their feet and cheers.

Eddie T walks onto the stage, different clothes but the same grungy look. Debra's girlfriends were not impressed, but as the crowd got silent and he began to sing they too became enraptured by his words and his voice. Debra stared at him with an intensity that he could feel. She tried to decipher his features; she tried to figure out what color his eyes were even though his hat was again pulled down over his eyes. She noticed he had facial hair that made his skin look almost dirty, yet his finger nails were perfect. Debra was mesmerized by this man and knew he would become her obsession.

As he finished his song, he looked toward Debra's table and her girlfriends began to wink, show cleavage and embarrass her. He made a quick head nod towards Debra's table and she waved back.

"You honestly think he's waving at you?" Christine chimed in and broke Debra's concentration. Maybe he wasn't addressing me she thought. He walked off the stage, but this time instead of disappearing behind a curtain, he walked off the left side of the stage and into the crowd. He made his way over to Debra's table, walked up behind Debra, and whispered in her ear, "I look forward to seeing you again." Debra froze, not knowing what to do or say. He walked away back into the crowd and Debra was left speechless.

"What did he say, girl?" That was Nicole being nosy, but the other women

followed up with the same question, one sounding more anxious than the other.

Debra lied and said, "Thanks for coming." She had remembered that same message being delivered to her the last time she had gone out with her girlfriends. "I look forward to seeing you". That was a different club, it couldn't possibly be the same guy, Debra thought.

After the nights' events, the women headed to the subways, where they would part ways at the first stop. Debra got off and waited on the platform for her train. As she stood there humming the words to Eddie T's song, someone walked up behind her.

"So, you like my song?" the stranger asked and instantly she knew it was Eddie. She felt her stomach tighten with nervousness but tried to remain calm. She turned around slowly, as if uninterested and

to her surprise that mysterious man who wore grungy clothing and his hat low over his eyes, was standing in front of her bare. Still wearing the Army jacket, but now the baseball hat was replaced with a beanie.

Debra was so astonished that she not only recognized the singer, but that she knew him personally. There he was standing there, looking like a totally different person. What a difference a hat and facial hair could make. It was 'little Tony'. She was at a loss for words.

"Don't look so surprised Deb." Tony said this with a slight grin on his face. He had never called her by her first name, let alone 'Deb'. She tried to gather herself and make sense of it all.

"Are you trying to tell me that you're the one I just saw singing on stage? You're Eddie T?" Debra was still in some what of a shock.

"Tony Edwards. Eddie T. Makes sense doesn't it? It's just a play on the name." Tony was speaking matter of factly as if the situation was no big deal. *"So pretty lady, where are you heading now?"*

"Anthony!" Debra said as if she wanted to maintain professionalism right there in the subway.

"What? We're both grown and we are definitely not in the office, are we?" For some reason Tony felt confident and secure at that moment. *"So, where are you headed?"*

Debra was still having a slightly difficult time wrapping her head around the situation. This was 'little Tony', the son of one of her closest friends. He was also Eddie T, the man who had made her melt speaking only six words in her ear.

"Umm, I'm on my way home," she said as she turned around and folded her

arms in front of her. She was disappointed. Her fantasy was now ruined. How could she fantasize about her friends' son? This was just her luck, she thought.

Just then her train pulled up, she hopped on with out speaking another word and stood facing the opposite direction. She hadn't realized that he had hopped on right along with her. She felt some one push against her slightly as the train rattled, but she thought nothing of it. She got off at her stop and walked up the stairs to street level.

"So, you live around here?" she heard Tony yell from behind her.

"Are you following me?" She said in a stern voice.

"Yes, I am." He shot back with a grin. "How about we grab a bite to eat?"

"Are you serious, Tony? You can't be serious." She felt the entire situation was inappropriate.

"Yes, I'm very serious. I know a nice little bar that serves food until 3. So, how about it?"

Debra was feeling hungry, but 'grabbing a bite to eat' with little Tony didn't sit well with her.

"I don't think so... I just don't think it would look, it's just not a good idea."

"So you're saying you and your employees have never eaten together?"

"I'm not saying that." Debra was feeling guilty but didn't want to be unprofessional.

"So what are you saying? I'm not good enough to eat with?" He chuckled.

"Okay, okay but quickly." Damn, he was insistent, Debra thought as he lead her to a bar close by. She couldn't believe she

lived right around the corner but she had never been there.

"Damn, this is amazing," Tony said, "I never would have thought in a million years, I'd be sitting here with you."

"I know the feeling, "Debra said in what seemed to be a more relaxed tone. They sat there at the bar eating and talking for what seemed like hours. The bartender pointed to his watch, letting them know they would be closing soon.

"So Debra, I think I've kept you against your will long enough. I'll walk you home and be on my way." They left the bar and headed towards Park Ave. Instinctively, he held her hand as they walked. For some reason, Debra didn't pull away and they walked hand in hand all the way to her front door. This was completely out of her character.

"Well, I must say that I am surprised that I didn't know there was a musician hiding inside you." Debra said with a relaxed smile. Jake did say he received a degree in performing arts.

"Yea, I know it crazy! You know what they say about artists…"

"They're unemployed!" they said in unison and began to laugh.

"Well, I'll let you get that beauty sleep even though we both know you don't need it."

"Thanks for the food, I appreciate it. Keep doing your music, you're very good at it." Debra said almost in a whisper as she felt herself blush. Tony leaned in slowly as if he was going to kiss her; he put his right hand on her cheek and whispered in her ear, "I look forward to seeing you." He kissed her on the cheek softly as he pulled himself away.

Debra was barely able to utter good night as he turned and began to walk away. She turned the key, but stopped to watch him for a second and suddenly he turned around and began walking back towards her.

He stopped so close to her she could feel the heat from his body. She didn't know what to do, so she waited. He stood staring intensely into her eyes and uttered the words 'fuck it' before he kissed her. He grabbed the back of her head with his left hand and pulled her body closer with his right. His lips were soft and moist. Debra was in shock again. He used his tongue to part her lips. Just as he did that she managed to pull herself out of the trance he had put her in.

"What are you doing?" She said with a tone of shock and excitement.

"I'm doing what I've wanted to do since I saw you in your office looking sexy

as hell behind that desk." Tony had passion and determination in his eyes.

"We can't do this," she said as she tried to take a step back, "this isn't right." She paused and looked at him staring back at her as if nothing she said mattered at that moment.

Tony grabbed her again and pressed her back up against the door. He kissed her again, with even more passion than the first time and their weight pushed the door open. She stood there looking at him and made a decision.

"Screw it." She whispered as she grabbed him and closed the door behind him. They kissed passionately and hurriedly as they began removing each others clothes. They tripped over her coffee table and landed on her love seat. Tony grabbed the back of her bra and with one swoop motion

it was laying on the floor next his shoes and her shirt.

"I'm going to make you feel so good," he said as he gently placed one of her breasts into his mouth. Instantly, Debra's body had chills. She knew that what she was doing was wrong, but he was doing all the right things and making all the right moves.

She could feel him kissing her stomach, her waist and then he removed her panties with his teeth and slipped his hot, wet tongue inside her. Her knees went weak and she began to slide lower. He grabbed her ass and asked, "How do you feel, baby?" She couldn't speak; her mind was in a daze. He rose up and over her and took her breasts into his mouth again.

She could hear him putting on a condom and she thought, 'this is my moment to stop the madness', but somehow he was able to put on the condom and maintain a physical connection with her, it almost seemed as if he had barely stopped touching her at all. When his eyes met hers again, they spoke volumes. He stared into her eyes unwaveringly as he entered her body. She felt his hot, throbbing manhood slide his way inside of her. 'Damn, he feels good', she thought to herself and she closed her eyes and ...let go.

They made love right there on her couch and several other places in her home in those wee hours of the morning. When they finally had their fill of one another, it was approaching 7a.m. They fell asleep in Debra's bed, with their bodies entangled.

Debra began to awaken and realized where she was and what had taken place. It was already 4p.m.

"Holy shit," she said as she jumped out of the bed hastily. "Get up! Get up!" She

yelled as she shook Tony. He woke with a smile on his face.

"Good morning sunshine," he said while reaching for her hand. She stepped back and covered herself with the sheet.

"You have got to go. I can't believe this. Oh my God!" She seemed nervous, upset and confused all at once.

"Relax, sweetie." Tony stood up in front of her, naked; his manhood standing slightly erect. She looked down at it and felt herself get a little aroused.

"Come here, what's wrong?" He took her into his arms and kissed her like it was a usual occurrence. She felt her body get warm all over again. He stroked her back and she could feel him getting even more erect.

He unfolded her arms and slowly slipped the sheet from around her body. Her nipples were fully erect and now so was his manhood. He placed her on the bed and began kissing her from head to toe. She rang her fingers through his hair and for a second she was lost in the moment again. As she began to feel him enter her body again, she fought the urge to let her body become one with his again. She pushed him and jumped up and out of the bed again.

"You have to leave. Please, you have to go." He was confused yet still aroused.

"Deb, relax. What's the problem?"

"You just have to go," she said as she ran around picking up his belongings. She felt embarrassed and ashamed. He followed her into the living room where they had made love only a few hours ago. She handed him his clothes and walked over to the door.

"You have to go now, you can't stay. You shouldn't have been here in the first place." She looked as if she had tears in her eyes and he was worried.

"Talk to me sweetie, tell me what's wrong?" He was really concerned, he had real feelings for this woman and didn't like seeing her unhappy.

"This was a one time thing, right? You think it's cool to screw your boss, right!" Debra now had anger in her voice. Tony was beginning to understand that she felt used and like he had taken her for a ride.

"I know you don't think I just wanted sex from you?"

"I don't know what you wanted, but you have to go," she said as she pushed him out. She closed the door and leaned against it as tears began to roll down her face.

"This is not how I wanted it to be, Deb. I care about you," he said from the other side as he knocked.

"Nancy, do I have anything big on my schedule today?" Debra asked her assistant hoping she'd be able to end the day early.

"No meetings, no calls. Looks like you have an empty day today," Nancy said with a chuckle, as it was rare that Mrs. Worthington had an empty day, "but Mr. Edwards, the colleague not the employee, did call and say he would be stopping by around noon. He said he'd bring lunch because he had a lot to talk to you about."

Debra didn't like the way Nancy enunciated 'a lot'. What did he have to talk about? Did Tony tell his father how unprofessional she had been? Debra tried to calm herself down by telling herself it was nothing. She decided to take a trip down to her finance department to speak with Tony rather than having him summoned to her office.

Since she was known to occasionally walk through one of her departments, she didn't think it would look suspicious. The employees would either think she was their to praise someone for a job well done, by giving out an award or visit someone who's work performance was in question.

As she entered the department, she could feel butterflies in her stomach. She wanted to seem as calm, cool, collected and as normal as possible. She was greeted by several employees. Debra did a quick survey of the cubicles and spotted Tony in what seemed to be a secluded corner on the far left side of the room. She spoke briefly with a few people who stopped to greet her and continued to make her way toward Tony.

When she arrived at his desk, he was standing there awaiting her arrival. He had watched her from the moment she entered the room. Debra could smell his captivating cologne and felt her loins tingle. She remained poised and professional as she knew that many of the other employees were still paying close attention.

"May I speak with you for a moment, Mr. Edwards?" Debra spoke with a confident unwavering voice that completely disguised her anxiety.

"Yea sure, but I don't have a private office or anything." Tony chuckled, trying to keep the mood light. He could sense her tension and wanted her to relax. She let out a forced laugh and gestured toward the meeting room located adjacent to his cubicle.

"Close the blinds please." Debra did not want any onlookers trying to read their lips while speaking with Tony in the all glass,

enclosed meeting room about their escapade two nights before.

After making sure the door was locked and the blinds were closed, Tony walked over to Debra and stopped just short of physical contact. He stood there staring into her eyes and waited for her to speak. This almost intimidated Debra as she had a flashback of that night she watched him perform and felt herself melt when he whispered in her ear.

"Ok, well I'm sure you know why I'm here." Debra was desperately trying to seem collected.

"You know what you need? You need to just relax some times. You're so uptight at work. You're going to stress yourself out."

"Listen, I don't know what came over me the other night. I don't remember drinking so, maybe I had a spell of temporary insanity or something, but in any

event it won't be happening again." Debra stepped back and turned around knowing that her body would try to contradict what her mind knew was best.

"I know this is a crazy situation for you to be in but the bottom line is that," he paused, walked over to Debra to regain eye contact before he continued, 'the bottom line is that I don't know how, but I know I want to be with you."

"You have got to be kidding me!" Debra then realized where she was and lowered her voice to a whisper. "I'm your boss. I'm good friends with your father. There's no way. This is insane."

Without saying another word, Tony kissed her just like he had every other time before that; with intensity and passion. He wrapped her up in his arms and she didn't push him away immediately. She found herself feeling warm, safe and renewed when she was near him. She refocused and removed herself from his grip, putting space between them once again.

"You can't sit here and tell me you don't feel something here, Deb?" Tony looked at her with wanting eyes as he reached for her hand.

"I heard what you said the other day I want you to know that I don't just want your body. I want all of you. All of your mind, spirit and even that 'gotta-be-tough' attitude you have sometimes. I know there's an age difference, but we have so much in common. That night I spent with you was unlike any other. It wasn't just about the love we made. We spoke for hours and hours before that even happened. I found myself intrigued by you. We shared a deeper part of ourselves with one another, deeper than just physical desires. I want you and I'm not going away."

Tony had a look on his face that told Debra he was serious and sincere in the words he spoke. She had to admit that she did feel something, but she couldn't quite say what exactly. She just knew it was there and that she wanted him too.

"I need to see you before you leave the office today," Debra said in a stern, almost irritated tone as they walked out of the meeting room. She was trying to seem as if the talk she had just had with Tony was one of professional significance.

Debra sat in her office replaying her encounter with Tony over and over again. She gave herself thousands of reasons why she shouldn't be with Tony, and then reasons why she should be with him came rushing into her mind. She thought about how she felt at that moment she first heard him singing, the sensation that ran through her body when he kissed her for the first time. Debra was feeling overwhelmed with emotions and feeling a little flush.

Months went by and Debra and Tony managed to keep their relationship a secret from those who they both knew. Debra found it amazing that some of her distant friends thought it was great that she had someone in her life that made her happy and that she shouldn't hide that happiness, yet when she mentioned the thought of dating a man Tony's age, her close friends said it would be insane of her to think it would ever be long term. Tony heard some criticism from some of his peers as well about how Debra would try to mother him and want to tie him down with marriage and children because her 'clock was ticking' but Tony felt and believed differently. He had grown to love the free and youthful spirit that Debra had and the fact that she never intimidated him with conversations of 'settling down'. Besides, Tony was not the typical man who was afraid of commitment.

They enjoyed weekends together cuddling at home or taking in a late show at a jazz café or Debra would tag along when he had a gig. She loved seeing him perform songs that he had written specifically for her or with her in mind. He had written songs about his love for her and the special bond they had developed. Things were going well for them and though the relationship remained a secret for some time, it was a decision they made together.

NINE MONTHS IN:

"Mrs. D, there is an Anthony Edwards here to see you", Nancy chimed over the intercom. She was beginning to wonder why Tony had been up to Mrs. Worthington's office on such a regular basis, but didn't see anything extraordinary standing out, so thought nothing more of it.

As Tony entered the office, he made sure to stay professional until the door was closed behind him and he was sure Nancy wasn't listening in. He walked over to Debra who was sitting at her desk facing the other way, watching the latest installment of Court TV. He stood right in front of her, blocking her view just staring at her.

"What is it baby? I'm watching my show." Debra had now become accustomed to Tony visiting her office from time to time, usually once every two months, at least that Nancy knows of. He had snuck up to see her

when Nancy was away from her desk on a few occasions.

"I got some news today from one of the labels I sent my demo to." His tone of voice was disappointed and frustrated and Debra readied herself to be the supportive girlfriend Tony had come to appreciate.

"Tell me what they said, sweetie. What did they say?"

"Well, they basically said... well, you know I've been trying to get signed for a long time now and it's getting old, you know."

Debra interjected, trying to encourage him to keep trying and to keep following his heart.

"Let me finish, Deb. The bottom line is that I don't think that I can continue working at a place like this, this isn't my dream. It drives me crazy to put this suit on every morning. This is your thing and you

do it well, but it's just not for me." He continued as Debra sat back in her chair and braced herself for what sounded like a resignation.

"So, you're quitting? What are you going to do? What is your plan?"

"Well baby, my plan is to follow my dreams...and go make music with this label that is ready to sign me today!" Tony exclaimed and Debra realized he was bluffing. She jumped into his arms and squeezed him tightly.

"Don't do that to me Tony! That's not funny; I thought you were really hurt and ready to give up." There was a big sigh of relief from Debra. They talked about how happy he was that after all his trials and numerous errors; he was finally going to make it big. They talked about which song would be the first single and what the album cover would look like.

"Damn baby, I have to say thank you so much for believing in me when everyone else said it was a waste of time. I really appreciate you for that. I love you."

"I love you too, Tony." Immediately they both realized that this was the first time either of them had uttered those words to one another. They had spoken about the importance of those three little words and vowed they wouldn't use it unless they meant it. There would be no 'throwing around' of the 'L' word.

Tony took Debra's face in his hands and looked passionately into her eyes.

"I love you Debra Worthington and there's no changing that."

With a shy smile on her face Debra realized that Tony had found his way into her heart as well.

"Well, I love you too and I don't want to change that."

Tony kissed her just as he always had, with passion and conviction and for the first time she reciprocated that same intense conviction. He felt her love in this kiss. As the kissed began to deepen and the touching began they moved to her sofa and continued their passionate kisses.

"Wait a minute, what are we doing, Tony? This is my office."

"So what? We never really christened it anyway." He smiled and kissed her gently on her neck. He began softly stroking her collar bone as he caressed her breast with one hand. She rubbed his shoulders, his back, and then ran her fingers through his hair. He slowly began removing her blouse as she slowly loosened his tie. Tony wanted to make love to this woman every time they he kissed her. He didn't want just a quickie.

He wanted to be inside of her in more ways than one. He not only wanted her body, but also her mind, heart and soul. He knew he was in love the second night he saw her at his show.

Debra was feeling the same things Tony felt. She was finally ready to let her heart be free and available. She was ready to give it away to this man with whom it was unthinkable to even be with. She loved the way he kissed her and held her in his arms. She loved the way he stared at her and made her blush. She loved the compassion he showed and the attention he always gave her no matter the situation. She wanted him.

They had been intimate countless times before, but this time felt different. They were on one accord and they both felt it. He took his time and she was in no rush either. She found herself surprised at how comfortable and relaxed she was, even though they were right there in her office.

Tony took one of her hands in his and intertwined their fingers as he licked and gently pulled her lips into his mouth. With her eyes closed, Debra could feel his nature rising and that made her wet. She wanted him and he knew it. He was turned on just by the fact that he had the ability to excite her.

Just as Tony began to remove her skirt, someone busted into her office. They were both in shock as they stared back into the face of Jacob Edwards.

Teaching 101

"Can anyone answer the question posed on page 82?" Asked Mr. Jayson Anderson, a new employee at the high school where he himself graduated.

He was known by most of his colleagues and even some members of the town's board of education. They were once teachers at FDR (Franklin D. Roosevelt) High and some had been teachers of his.

He was an athlete in school and received both academic and sport scholarships for college. He worked hard to get into college, as he knew he would be the first in his family to attend and possibly graduate from college. His parent and other siblings had either dropped out of high school or joined the work force right after graduation.

Now here he was, an educated and well respected black man with a promising career and a reputation that preceded him.

"Mr. Jay, I can answer the question," said an overly confident 17 year old boy with a reputation for being the center of attention, "it's obvious to me what the answer is."

Jayson taught 12th grade history and all his students, even the ones seemingly unconcerned with school found themselves intrigued by this man who made history interesting.

Jayson was six feet four inches tall with smooth dark skin and piercing light brown eyes that seemed out of place within the dark tones of his complexion. He was slender, but toned and maintained his physique even after the injury that took him out of the running to become a professional basketball player.

~The Beginning Of The End~

Jayson grew up in a small town outside of Richmond, VA but he had big city dreams and decided that once he received his degree in history he would move to Baltimore to pursue a teaching career. He thought it would be rewarding and fulfilling to aid inner city youth in bettering themselves.

"I know this is your first day, but I am more than confident that you will be just fine. These kids are just looking for some guidance. If you need anything, you let me know okay?" That was the voice of the assistant principal, Mr. Marcello Ambrosia

an ex football player in his late thirties, who just couldn't get over the fact that he was let go after his rookie year on an NFL team and was now obsessed with working out and training.

"Well, thank you Mr. Ambrosia. I definitely appreciate it. I won't let you down."

"Don't be so formal, call all me Marc. I want my teachers to feel comfortable. We go by first names around here." He gave Jayson a pat on the back as he showed him the door to the class he would now be teaching.

Luckily Jayson had the charm and charisma to help him get through the tough first few weeks. Once he became familiar with the types of attitudes he had to deal with, he knew what approach to take with each of his students.

Jayson was doing well and received a lot of praise from his fellow co-workers on how well he interacted with the students. The students loved him and paid attention to him when he spoke. They felt he could relate to them because he was so young.

The end began for Jayson when Isis Montanez transferred from a high school in New York City. She was 18 years old and she had a Halle Berry face, with a Beyonce body. She was Jamaican and Portuguese and Jayson knew he would have a problem from the moment she stepped into his classroom.

Jayson was told by Marc that he would be getting a new student and she should be in class by the time he showed up on Monday morning. When Jayson showed up for his 8:25 class she was already there, sitting in the far right corner of the room fiddling with her cell phone. She seemed not to be the least bit bothered by the fact that other students were standing around whispering about her arrival.

"Good morning, guys. I want to introduce our newest student, Isis." Jayson said as he gestured over to the corner where she sat. "Would you please stand up and tell us where you're from and a little bit about yourself?" As she stood up, the room fell silent. No one had realized her beauty. Her features were strong, yet feminine and she had skin like flawless butterscotch. She was 5' 8 and very curvy. She looked around the room as everyone anticipated hearing her speak for the first time.

"Well, my name is Isis as you already know, I'm 18 and I'm from Brooklyn. If there's anything else ya wanna know, you're just gonna have to come ask me yourself."

She said with her heavy New York accent, and then she sat down without missing a beat. Everyone was in awe including Jayson. He was captured by her beauty, her sensually raspy voice and the way she carried herself. Jayson quickly gathered himself.

"Well Isis, if there is anything you need feel free to ask me."

From the opposite corner of the room came a low whisper, "I got all you need right here, baby girl" Said one of the male students.

Isis heard the comment and without looking up replied, "I don't mess with little boys."

Jayson went on with the lesson for that day but found he had difficulty keeping the boys in class from making sexually explicit comments. The class ended, but not soon enough for Jayson. As everyone exited, he saw that Isis remained seated.

"Is something wrong? Do you need help finding your next class?"

"No. I just wanted to talk to you for a quick minute, if that's ok with you?" She asked in her sensual voice.

"Ok, shoot. What's up?" Jayson shuffled some papers on his desk to seem uninterested and busy. She stood and walked over to his desk and stood next to him. Too close for Jayson's comfort, but he remained cool. She was standing over him and he could smell her jasmine perfume.

"I know this is gonna sound a little bit crazy, but I'm only asking you because you're the youngest teacher I've seen here and I definitely can't ask these little boys and girls."

Jayson braced himself for a question that might make him uncomfortable.

"What is it?"

"Well, being that I'm legal," Oh no, here it comes Jayson thought to himself, *"I want to know where the good clubs are. You look like you might check out a club here and there, so what's up?"*

Jayson was caught off guard by the question and almost didn't know what to say. "Don't you think you should be focused on school or hanging out with your 'girls' or whatever you kids do?"

"First of all Jayson, I am a woman. Second of all, I'm a straight A student and beyond that, I don't 'hang out' with little girls." Jayson could hear the attitude in her voice but she remained cool and collected. Not once had she adjusted her stance or seemed uneasy. "I take it you're not gonna answer my question? Ok, fine. I'll find out from some else." She said as she sashayed out the door in a steady controlled pace.

Jayson exhaled as he sat back in his chair and hoped he wouldn't have any issues with this New Yorker, who inappropriately, turned him on.

Three months went by and everyone had returned from winter break with newly lifted spirits and enthusiasm about the end of the school year. Jayson had become fairly close to Marc and they spent time together on occasion. When they hung out, it was usually at Marc's apartment or at a bar.

Marc stopped by Jayson's classroom Friday afternoon as Jayson was packing up for the day.

"Hey man, feel like checking out this club that just opened up downtown? I hear that's where all the ladies are hanging out now a days. I think it's called Blue Lake, Blue Water, Blue something. How 'bout it?"

Jayson had heard of the place, but wasn't sure he was in the mood for a club that night.

"I've heard of it, it's called Blu Lagoon I think but I don't know...maybe next week or something."

"Come on man, no school Monday. Plus we haven't hung since before break. Let's go out and find some ass, man."

"Marc, I don't look for ass." Before Jayson could continue Marc interjected, "Right, because the ass just comes to you." They both laughed and Jayson finally agreed to go but only if Marc promised not to embarrass him.

They arrived at Blu Lagoon at around 11:30 and there was a short line outside which made Jayson rethink his decision to accompany Marc out that night. When they entered the club, they were both impressed by the atmosphere. The club was nowhere

near as small as it seemed from the outside.
It had huge floor to ceiling columns had a
Roman feel. In the center of the first room
was a small lagoon, hence the name, with
royal blue water and blue lighting around it.

"Damn, would you look at that shit? I
ain't ever seen something like this before!"
Marc was clearly impressed. Jayson
thought the lagoon mixed with the Roman
theme was pretty cool too.

They finally made their way to the bar
which would have been a much shorter walk
if Marc didn't feel the need to throw out
some insane line to every other female he
saw on the way to the bar.

They sat at the bar for a while
shooting the breeze, talking about work, the
women at work, the female students who
looked like grown women and other random
things.

"Jay, I think that chick on the other side of the bar is trying to get your attention."

"What?" Jayson was not paying too much attention to the women in the club. He would smile at a few who he thought were fairly attractive, but there weren't any that he saw, that he thought was worth conversation.

"Look to your left, over by the hallway entrance. She's sitting at the end. I think she's trying to get your attention." Jayson took a quick glance and noticed the woman Marc was refereeing to. She was indeed trying to get his attention. As soon as he looked, she stood up and smiled as if she was getting ready to approach him. He looked back at Marc and said, "Man please. That chick is too thirsty."

"What! Are you kidding me? What the hell is that supposed to mean?"

"It means... I'm not into chicks that beg for my attention, and then act all shy. Either you know what you want and you go get it, or you don't do anything and hope it will come to you."

"She was trying to get your attention, isn't that going after it enough?"

"If she wanted to speak to me, she would have just come over to me."

"Man, you're full of shit. Go talk to that chick man, you said you would be mellow tonight. Come on, go over there." Jayson knew that Marc could be not only persistent, but that persistence could turn into utter annoyance, so he decided to over to the female.

As he got up to leave, he noticed the woman stood up, began to walk toward the hallway, then turned and gestured for him to follow her. Jayson immediately regretted even looking in her direction.

He followed the woman into the hallway where she stopped in front of the bathroom door.

"Hi, what's your name?" She said, trying to sound sexy. Jayson did feel that she was attractive but she was trying a bit too hard for his liking.

"Mike," he said without hesitation. He made it a habit not to tell women he wasn't interested in his real name. He had had some crazy stalker issues in the past and had learned his lesson.

"I must say, you had my attention as soon as you sat down." 'Is that so?' Jayson thought to himself. He wouldn't have noticed her if Marc hadn't pointed her out.

"So, what's up?" He asked in calm relaxed voice, as if he wasn't already bored with the female.

She leaned into him pressing his back against the wall and whispered in his ear, "I want to taste you," she said in an almost begging voice. Jayson jerked back, looked her in the face and saw that she was not joking. She had one hand on his belt, and the other was stroking his tool, all while she tried to edge him into the bathroom. He gently pushed her back, fixed his buckle and walked away without a word.

He sat back down at the bar to an eagerly waiting Marc, who was ready to hear the details. Marc was sure that Jayson had gotten her number and would be getting much more later on that night.

"So, what happened? What did she say?" Marc asked anxiously like a toddler awaiting their favorite bedtime story.

"Nothing. I told you that chick was thirsty." Jayson said as he began to get up once again. He decided he needed a change of scenery as soon as he spotted that same female walking back from where he had just

come from; with a man following close behind, touching her ass.

"What?! What the hell! Man, did you get the digits or what?"

"That chick told me she wanted to suck my dick." Jayson uttered disgustedly.

"Are you serious? Man, you're crazy. Stop lying. You're just mad cause she changed her mind about giving you her number once see saw you up close." Marc joked.

"I'm serious." Jayson stared at Marc with a straight face indicating he was definitely not playing.

"Damn, for real? I would have let her suck me dry." Marc reeled in the idea.

"I don't think so, chicks like that come with STD's and that's something I definitely can do without." Jayson left making his way into another part of the club. He was headed over to the lounge

section, to try and relax and get his mind off of that nasty female.

As he entered the room, he immediately felt a calm come over him. There were a few people mingling and even a few dancing, but most of the people in this room were just sitting around chatting. He went to the bar and ordered another drink. As he leaned against the bar waiting for his drink, he took in the vibe. The bar tender handed him his drink and as he began to make his way to an open seat with a nice view of the game, he was bumped by two females on their way towards the bar.

He looked up and saw a very attractive Hispanic female with a smile as big as her curly black hair.

"I'm so sorry," She said with an accent that was Spanish with a New York flare, "I didn't see you, I guess I wasn't paying attention." Just as she finished her

sentenced the other young lady stood up after picking up her purse which had fallen to the ground during the collision. Jayson couldn't believe his eyes, it was Isis and boy did she look like a woman. Any ideas he had had about getting the other woman's phone number were completely erased at that moment.

"Well, well, well. Look who we have here," Isis said as she put a hand on one of her curvy hips.

"Uh, hey. What are you doing here?" Jayson was in shock but tried to appear cool.

"Girl, where do you know this fine ass man from?" Her friend questioned, wanting a formal introduction.

"Around." She said still looking directly at Jayson. She had to admit, the man was fine. She could tell that her friend was more than interested so decided to

introduce them. If she didn't, she knew her friend would bring it up continuously.

"Shae'la this is Jayson, Jayson meet my friend from back home, Shae'la."

They shook hands and exchanged pleasantries. Jayson was still unsure of what to say or do, so he decided the best thing to do was get out of that awkward situation.

"Well, it was nice meeting you Shae'la," he shook her hand again and said, "See you around Isis." He winked at her and began to walk away. He got about two steps away when he felt a tug on his arm. He stopped and there she was staring up at him, once again way too close for comfort.

She leaned into him and whispered in his ear, "I saw that little situation you had in the hallway," Jayson was surprised and slightly embarrassed that she had witnessed that, "if I wasn't the lady I am, I might try the same thing." She licked the tip of his ear discreetly and walked off with her girlfriend.

Monday morning came and Jayson was apprehensive about seeing Isis in his classroom. He arrived early and tried to give himself a pep talk about not paying her any attention, acting like he didn't see her at the club, and most of all trying to get the thoughts he was having out of his head. What she did when she licked his ear isn't something that was unfamiliar to Jayson, but he felt guilty about having sexual thoughts about one of his students.

The bell rung and the student began filing in. Jayson received his usual 'hello's and good mornings'. The second bell rung and Jayson realized that he hadn't seen Isis come in. He was somewhat relieved, yet he wondered what had happened to her. Could something have happened to her at the club? He pushed his whirling thoughts out of his head long enough to get through his classes for the day.

After his last class which ended at 1 p.m. Jayson decided he would stay later than the usual, since it was easier for him to focus while still at school rather than at home.

He sat there grading papers and reviewing the next days' lesson. Thoughts of Isis kept coming in and out of his mind. Suddenly he heard a knock at the door. Marc walked in as if he had some exciting news. He pulled up a chair in front of Jayson's desk, leaned forward on his elbows and stared at Jayson.

"Are you going to say something or are you waiting for me to act like I give a shit?" Jayson chuckled as he put his papers down.

"Man, I need to tell you something. I shouldn't be telling you, but I gotta tell somebody or else I'm gonna lose my mind." Marc was dead serious; the usual youthful tone of his voice was not there. Marc had Jayson's undivided attention.

"What's up, man? Tell me what's going on?'

"Ok. You know the secretary, Michelle that works here a few days a week?"

"Yea, what about her?"

"Well, she has been bugging me to take her out for the longest time now, so I finally decided to do it. So we go to a movie and afterwards we head over to that late night café on Madison. Everything is going good and I'm pretty sure she's gonna give it up to me so I work my magic and she invites me back to her place."

"Sounds good, sounds good. Where's the problem?"

"Well, we head over to her place and you know we're getting hot and heavy on her couch. She tells me she wants me, but we gotta be quiet because her younger sister is there. I'm thinking fine, no problem. I've done chicks with their husbands in the other room."

"You know you ain't right Marc. One of these days, you're gonna get shot."

"So listen, I tell her I need to use the bathroom. I go into the bathroom, handle my business and as I'm sneaking back out, because you remember the sister is there, who do I run into?!" Jayson knew this was a rhetorical question and was almost sure of the answer.

"The sister!"

"The sister?" Jayson asked.

"Yea, the sister. She grabs me and leads me back into the bathroom by my Johnson. Can you believe that shit?!Then she sticks her tongue down my throat."

Jayson was shocked and didn't really know how to respond, so he just continued to listen, but Marc paused instead waiting for Jayson to respond. It began to click in Jayson's mind where the problem was.

"Damn, is that the same Michelle that has a little sister named Nikki that goes to this school... Man you gotta be out of your fucking mind! You didn't go any further than that did you?"

"Oh God man, what am I gonna do?" That was basically Marc's affirmation that he had had sex with Nikki. "I tried to push her away, but I didn't want to make a huge commotion and get Michelle all involved." Jayson was in shock.

"Yo man, don't tell me anymore. I don't want to hear it. Why are you telling me this? This is some crazy shit."

"Who else can I tell? I don't want to lose my job, but I had to tell somebody."

"When did this happen?"

"Last weekend."

"Whoa, hold up. Wait a minute. The same night we went out to the club?" Jayson was tripping out and didn't know what to think. He didn't know if he wanted to hear more or if he should just get up and leave.

"No, the weekend before that. It's just that I thought I could just pretend like it didn't happen, and avoid her and her sister at all cost. Then at the Blu Lagoon, I thought I saw one of your students and it tripped me out. I just couldn't hold it anymore."

Jayson's mind quickly jumped to Isis, and he wondered if Marc had seen the brief encounter. He was doing well in Baltimore as a teacher and didn't want to lose his job over something like this. He ignored Marc's comment and tried to focus.

"Oh man, this is crazy. I can't believe you did that... Shit!"

"Yea, I know man. It was crazy and I ran into her in the hallway the other day and I almost had a heart attack. She walked up to me and said, 'Hey Mr. Ambrosia', all sweet and sexy and shit. I know it wasn't right, but man that little girl knew what the hell she was doing. If she wasn't..." before he could continue, Jayson stopped him.

"Marc, focus man. You could lose your job if someone found out about this. What if she talks?"

"Man I don't know. I don't know. Now I'm scared to brush Michelle off cause I don't know what her sister may or may not have told her."

Two weeks went by and neither Marc nor Jayson mentioned their conversation again. Things in Jayson's classroom seemed to have gotten back to normal or so he thought.

It was Friday afternoon and Jayson was packing up for the day when Marc walked in.

"What's up man? What you got planned for the weekend?" Marc asked in voice that clearly expressed his party mood, but Jayson was not feeling that.

"I'm not getting into anything tonight, man. I'm just gonna go home, grade some papers and chill out. Maybe next weekend."

"Come on man, let's go out. I need to get wasted."

"I don't think so. When you get wasted, I end up having to make sure you

don't choke on your vomit. I'd rather not tonight." Jayson showed no sign of being persuaded so Marc realized his defeat and left.

As Jayson grabbed the last of his belongings and began to walk toward the door and in walked none other than Isis Montanez. 'Oh shit', Jayson thought to himself.

"Hello, Jayson. Haven't seen you at the Lagoon since that night, what's up with that? Don't you want to see me?" She asked in a low, intimate tone.

"Is there something I can do for you? Don't you have a class or something?" Jayson tried to sound professional without sounding uncomfortable or defensive.

"Well no, I don't have a class or something. You did say that if I needed anything I could come to you, right? Or was

that just some bullshit you're taught to say?"

"No it wasn't bullshit. So, what's up?" Jayson was sincerely concerned. His students knew they could talk to him about anything, sometimes Jayson himself was surprised at how personal some of the students got.

Isis walked over to him and sat on the edge of his desk. There she was again, always invading his personal space. She sat staring at him long enough to make him squirm.

"So, are you gonna tell me what it is that you need or are you waiting for me to guess?" He said in a joking manner, trying to lighten the mood and distract her from his nervousness.

"You would never be able to guess what it is that I need from you." She responded with a very sexy tone. She had

been having sexual fantasies about Jayson since the first day she entered his classroom. She loved his chocolate skin, his physique and the fact that his lips always looked ready for a kiss, never mind his intelligence.

"So, what is it? Spit it out."

"I'm working on this website and I want your opinion on it."

"Ok. Which subject it for? Maybe that teacher would be able to give you better feedback."

"It's not for a class, it's personal. I'm getting into the entertainment industry and I have a webpage with my pictures, samples of my music and bio information. I just need to know if it would be appealing to a random person passing by or maybe even an agent. So, do you mind checking it out and letting me know what you think?"

Jayson was slightly hesitant, but quickly decided it wouldn't do any harm to just check it out and give her some constructive criticism.

"Ok, I think I handle that."

"But can you handle me," She said under her breath. Jayson heard the comment and instantly had sexual thoughts about her but he quickly pushed them out of his mind.

Saturday evening rolled around and Jayson had already taken a shower after his weekly basketball game at the park. He decided that since he had graded all the papers he had taken home, he would pack up his briefcase, so everything would be ready to go on Monday morning.

As he began to clean out his briefcase he came across the small piece of paper that Isis had written her website information on. He set it to the side deciding he would get to it later.

Jayson settled in on his couch to watch ESPN and realized he had already seen all the games they were highlighting that evening and wasn't quite interested in the others. He decided to check out the website.

Jayson was astonished upon entering the site. Across the top were the words 'Isis: More Than A Goddess' in bold red letters. The website looked very professional, as did her pictures. There were different poses and outfits. In some she looked her age, very youthful and innocent. In other pictures she looked like an experienced, grown woman.

Jayson browsed the site and was about to leave, when the promise he had made to give his feedback came to mind. He clicked on the button that said 'Leave A Comment' and in it he wrote: "Hi. I stopped by like I promised I would. So here's my feedback. The pictures were great, the bio was a bit brief; doesn't say much about you, but all-in-all the entire website looks very professional. If you did that all by yourself, you did a good job. Hope my input was helpful, J."

Jayson navigated away from her website hoping, he would be able to get those images of her in lingerie out of his head. He checked a few other website and finally decided to check his email. When he opened up his email, he found there were three emails with 'More Than A Goddess' in the subject line.

The first email was basic and pretty much said thank you for visiting the site. The second email was similar and said thanks for leaving your comment. Both seemed generic, like they had been automatically sent. The third one was from Isis herself and it read:

'I see that you are a man of your word. I can appreciate that from a man. Thanks for the feedback, I will try to improve my bio and hopefully it will make me that much more appealing to agents.

Anyway, I know I shouldn't be saying this because of the position you are in (...you can't even imagine the positions I'd like to be in with you) but I just have to say this. I know you see me watching you and it isn't simply because I love history class. I am woman enough to admit that I want you and I want you badly. I know you're the teacher here, but I've been thinking about the things I could teach you.

I see the way you look at me, I see the way you try to be cool when I get too close. I know you want to do things with and to me too. I can't believe I'm saying all these things to you, but I'm grown so I can tell you that I'm digging you. I know that if we were under difference circumstances we would be all over each other. You know it too.

Well, I guess I have 'crossed the line' enough for one day so I will leave it at that. I would suggest that we meet in secret, but I don't think you would go for that. Plus I wouldn't want to jeopardize your career.

Thanks again, for the feedback.

---Isis, your goddess ☺"

Jayson was shocked, amazed, confused and aroused all at the same time. He didn't know what to think or do. Should he respond or should he just let it go. His mind was telling him to just leave it alone, but somewhere deep inside was the urge and curiosity to get to know this girl. He wrote back:

'No problem. I told you when I first met you that if you needed anything, you

could come to me and that was no bullshit. I am a man of my word, so I did what I said I would.

I would just like to say good luck with your career in the entertainment industry. I see you have real talent as well as the looks.

Now as for the other things you said in your email...I will just say thanks for the compliment. You are right; I do have a career to think about. Well, I've gotta go but once again; if you need any other advice or anything else I will be more than happy to help.

-Jay'

Jayson wanted to be supportive but he loved his career and didn't want to lose his job. He thought the email he sent back was friendly but felt it didn't leave much room for Isis to go any further.

He left his computer and tried to find something to watch on television. He made himself something to eat and cozied up on his couch to watch another remake of "The Amityville Horror", a movie he loved.

Just as the movie was ending he heard a 'ding' come from his computer indicating that he had received a new email message. It was from Isis and it read:

'If I asked you for what I really wanted, I'm not so sure you would oblige. They say avoidance is a sign of fear and you avoided the things I said about us wanting each other. Are you afraid of me? Don't be scared, sweetheart. I won't bite, unless you want me to.

I want to get to know you Jayson. Is that against the rules?'

Jayson was once again conflicted. It was already too late to turn back now. He had opened the door by replying to her first message.

Needless to say, that Isis and Jayson continued their correspondences for the next two months. In that time, Jayson found out that Isis was living with a roommate, the same female she was with at the club when he ran into them. Isis asked that her schedule be changed so she would no longer have Jayson as her teacher. That was something she decided was best and he agreed.

They had become quite close and had learned quite a bit about one another. They were falling for each other, even though they had only spent time together on a few occasions at Isis' apartment when Shae'la was out of town.

Jayson would park his car three blocks away in a restaurant or shopping plaza parking lot, and then walk to her place.

Though they had had several instances where they had become physical, they never had sex. Jayson was determined not to go there until she had graduated. After all, he was already in the wrong.

It was a rainy Friday afternoon and Isis had stopped by after Jayson's last class on her way to work. Jayson was sitting at his desk trying to grade papers.

"Hey, sweetie. I'm heading to work, but since we have plans tonight I wanted to ask you if you could pick up the food on your way over?" Isis had become so comfortable that it was like they were in a full blown relationship. It pretty much was, because neither of them was seeing anyone else nor were they interested in seeing anyone else.

"Yea, no problem baby. About what time will you be home?" They were speaking as if this type of situation was normal.

"I'm leaving early because I want to spend all night with you." She said in a sexy tone as she winked an eye.

"Alright, well how about grabbing some movies from Blockbuster after you leave work?" Jayson was accustomed to her sly remarks, so he usually ignored them when he was at work.

Isis walked over to him and sat on his lap.

"What are you doing, girl? What if someone walks in and sees you on my lap?" Jayson was still very paranoid about being caught.

"I know, I know. I just wanted to give my baby a kiss before I left for the day. Is that so wrong?"

"Of course not, baby." They kissed
gently at first, then it became intense. They
embraced passionately and Isis decided to
straddle him. She started grinding her hips
as her grabbed her ass for dear life.

"Damn baby, I want you so bad." Isis
was dying to feel him inside of her, but she
knew he had his mind made up about
waiting until after the school year was
finished.

They kissed and kissed until Jayson
couldn't take it anymore. He grabbed her
and lifted her off of him.

*"Stop it, girl. Damn, we can't do that.
And we damn sure can't do that here."*

She grabbed his dick and pulled him
closer to her, then kissed him again. She
unbuttoned her jeans and put his left hand
down into her panties.

*"You feel that, baby. You see how
badly you got me yearning?"*

"Shit, girl! You're driving me crazy."
Jayson said in a low whisper.

Isis sat him back down in his chair
and straddled him again, this time allowing
his dick to penetrate her. She slid onto it
slowly and they both let out a silent breath.
Jayson couldn't believe what they were
doing and he couldn't believe how good she
felt.

Isis had been wanting to feel him
inside of her since the day she walked into
his classroom and finally she had him.

"Damn. This was worth the wait,
baby. You feel so good to me." She said as
Jayson suddenly jumped.

"Did you hear that?" Isis was so in
the groove she hadn't heard anything.

"Isis, I think someone is coming. Get
up. Get up!" He buttoned his pants and
fixed his shirt.

From the hallway they could hear Marc calling out to Jayson.

"Hey Jay, what's say we head out tonight man?"

Marc was coming down the hallway and fast. Jayson shuffled Isis over to the closet.

"Get in here and stay as quiet as possible. Don't even breathe loud." Isis hurried in, not wanting her man to lose his job. She realized she loved him and would do anything for him. Even hide out in classroom coat closets.

Marc walked into the room cheerfully and quite upbeat.

"What's up my man? What are you getting into tonight?" Marc was ready to party.

"I've got papers to grade and I promised someone I'd spend some time with them."

"Oh, so you've got some pussy waiting on you somewhere this weekend, huh? No time for little 'ol me?" Marc said in playful tone, before he continued. "Shit, if I had plans to get some pussy, I wouldn't be hanging out with me either." He laughed a hearty laugh for about one minute. Jayson didn't find the joke as amusing. He stood there waiting for Marc to speak.

"Alright my man, since you won't hang out with me tonight. How about we go grab a drink or two down on Lafayette before you go curl up in that pussy?"

"Alright, that's sounds reasonable. Let me grab my things and I'll meet you in the parking lot." Jayson was trying to get Marc out of his classroom so he could help Isis escape, but Marc wasn't going for it.

"I'm ok, I can wait for you." He just stood there, almost as if he knew Jayson was hiding something.

They began to walk out off the door and Jayson, tried to figure out what to do. As they began walking down the hallway Jayson stopped suddenly near an exit.

"Go on man, I forgot something in my room. I'll be down in a second." Jayson quickly walked off, not giving Marc a chance to respond. Marc stood in the middle of the hallway, waiting for a bit, and then slowly started walking back toward Jayson's classroom.

Jayson reached his classroom door and pulled it shut behind him as he entered. He walked over to the closet and Isis handed him his coat, as if she knew he'd be returning for it.

"Marc is in the hallway waiting for me. Wait here for a little while. I will send you a text when it is safe for you to leave, okay baby?" Jayson was nervous and she could tell.

"Don't worry baby, I'll wait for the signal. I would never do anything to mess with your career. I love you too much." She was surprised she had spoken those words out loud as if it were customary. They had both thought of saying them to one another before, but only in a passing thought. Jayson, almost instinctively responded the same way.

"I love you too, baby. See you tonight. Remember, wait for the signal." Jayson kissed her one more time and quickly closed the closet door as he heard Marc turning the doorknob. Jayson turned around and was standing by his desk before Marc opened the door.

"I'm ready man, let's go. I just forgot my jacket and a few papers." Jayson hoped that Marc hadn't seen Isis or their episode earlier, which he hadn't.

They walked out of the classroom door and there stood a janitor right in front of the classroom door directly across from Jayson's. Jayson's heart fell to his feet as the old man, he had never really paid much attention to, winked an eye at him. Jayson knew immediately that the little old man had seen the entire escapade or at least his trip back to the closet door through the window in his door. Either way, Jayson knew there would be trouble just by the way the old man winked and smirked at him.

That was the last drink Jayson and Marc ever had together. The following Monday Jayson turned in his letter of resignation without much of an explanation.

He moved to Teaneck, NJ and found himself another teaching job, only this time he chose middle school. He felt less pressure teaching that age.

The move seemed random to most, but as luck would have it Isis got herself a role on a New York City based TV show. By the start of the following school year, they had moved in together.

About a year later while sitting on the couch in their new apartment Jayson and Isis were making plans to take a trip to Aruba, when her show finished shooting. The phone rang but Jayson didn't move.

"Aren't you going to get that, baby?" Isis asked.

"If I'm not mistaken, you live here too." He replied with a grin, indicating he was no longer quite so paranoid about being open about their relationship. She jumped up and ran toward the phone, then quickly ran back. First she stared lovingly into his eyes and then kissed him.

"I love you too." He said to her knowing exactly what she was trying to express.

"Hello," She answered the phone hesitantly, being that it was her first time.

"Yea, I think I might have dialed the wrong number. I'm looking for Jayson Anderson."

"You've got the right number, would you like to speak with him?"

"Yes, I would. May I ask who I'm speaking with?"

"This is Isis and who am I speaking with?"

"Tell him it his old friend Marc." He said with a laugh. Isis' became silent as she turned to look at Jayson.

"Who is it, baby? Why do you look like that? Is it a bill collector?" Jayson laughed, but realized her expression didn't

change. He got up and took the phone from her.

"Hello, who is this?"

"It's Marc, remember me?"

Bite the Bullet

I've been working as a corrections officer for eleven years and never have I encountered a situation like the one I'm about tell you about.

My name is Andrea Wright and I started doing this only because when I graduated high school, I realized that most employers only hired people with degrees and I wasn't trying to work at McDonalds. I needed a job that would pay my bills and offer good benefits.

When I signed up to take the exam, they all said I would never pass. When I was called to start training, they all said I would never finish. When I started working, they all said I wouldn't make it one week, especially working in a male prison.

I've been at this institution for the past seven years and I have more than put in work.

March 3, 2000

A bus load of new inmates arrived two hours before my shift ended. I was working over at intake and so, these guys became my problem.

Everything went smoothly that night, but the next night a few members of that same group began starting trouble. People were trying to move in on other inmates and claim their territory.

There was Marquis Johnson, convicted of several charges including; assault with a deadly weapon, illegal possession of a concealed weapon, intent to commit bodily harm, verbal and physical assault of a police officer among other charges. Marquis AKA MJ was a

Philadelphia native who spent a lot of his youth in and out of juvenile facilities. He was built like a line backer, but just desired to fit in. He was like a big teddy bear, in a sense. He was mainly known as a 'stick up kid' with a trigger happy finger.

There was Tyson Dubois AKA Ty a thin guy with a quiet temperament. He was a follower, not a leader. He was born and raised in Newark, NJ and had already done a 3 year bid in his late teens. He was known for auto theft and was once again convicted for the same offense.

There was the mild and well mannered leader of the group named Domingo Justice. Funny last name for a man with a record, right? Dom as his peers called him was the one with the brains. He planned everything and was good at. He was from Bronx, NY. He was convicted of conspiracy to commit murder, fraud, aggravated assault and verbal and physical assault of a law enforcement officer. His sentence would not be as long as the others', because had it not been for the assault charges, he would only be on probation. The courts didn't really have much to go on regarding the conspiracy and fraud charges, nor did they really have much to go on with the so-called assault, but they had something to prove.

The trio became very popular within three months of their arrival. Domingo planned the 'take-overs' and MJ and Ty would carry out his orders exactly as he commanded.

Domingo had a large following of individuals by the fourth month he was there. The unique thing about his character is that he was genuinely respected, rather than merely feared by his 'workers'.

July 15, 2000

I was asked to escort Tyson to his weekly counseling session. When we arrived, his counselor, Ms. Carter was not in. I assumed she had just run out to the restroom. So, I decided to wait for a few moments.

"Looks, like we're going to have to wait for a little bit, but if she doesn't show up soon, we're going back to the yard." I gestured for him to take a seat in one of the chairs and he did.

He acted like he was a thug when he was around the other guys, but when he was around me or any other female staff, he was mild mannered, even soft spoken. At times he seemed almost timid.

We sat there in silence for almost ten minutes, before a word was spoken. He was moving around and fiddling with the tail of his shirt.

"Do you need to use the restroom, Tyson?" I asked in a slightly annoyed tone of voice.

"No ma'am, but I wish Ms. Carter would get here." He responded anxiously.

"She'll be here soon, just relax yourself okay."

"Can I ask you something?"

"What is it?" I asked not expecting the question that followed.

"Well, I'm curious...or should I say my boy Dom is curious. Do you have a man?"

"Now you know better than to be asking me those types of questions, right?" I responded in a stern voice. I had gotten come-ons before, but once they see that you won't play into it, they just drop it or make

sly comments but with nothing really behind it.

"I know but he made me promised to find out, so that's what I'm doing."

"Well, drop it." I said with my eyebrows raised indicating that I was not trying to hear it.

Five more minutes passed and I was getting annoyed. I had paperwork to do and I didn't feel sitting in this tiny room with Tyson.

"Alright man, I think we've waited long enough. You're just going to have to get rescheduled." I said as I took his arm.

"Wait a minute; I need to get something off my chest. Damn! I can't believe she's not here." He sounded upset, anxious and somewhat disappointed.

"Well, what do you what me to do? Do I look like the counselor?" I was not

trying to have any issues this week. It had been going so well, besides I was ready to get back to my pile of paperwork.

"Please, please just listen to me for two seconds. I promise it won't be long. And if you could just tell Ms. Carter for me that I need some advice, that would be cool. You'll probably see her before I do anyway."

I hesitated for a minute and tried to figure out if I should just let him speak so that I could get back to the work in my office.

"Ok, this is the deal" he started, lowering his tone, "I have a little dilemma." Here we go, I thought to myself. He is about to start telling me his little problems thinking I give a damn, but if I act like I do, we'll be out of here much quicker.

He continued, sitting back down "I kinda like somebody, but I don't know how to tell him." He said as he crossed his legs.

Oh my God, Tyson is a faggot! Do the others in his crew know? Are they homos too? This is some nasty shit!

"Alright stop! I don't want to hear anymore. You can wait till next week when you get to talk to Ms. Carter."

"No, just listen to my problem and give me your honest opinion. Woman to woman just let me know what you think." *Did this fruit cake just say 'woman to woman'? Oh hell no!*

"Well, um okay I guess I can help you out, but you've got to hurry up and tell me what the problem is. Then you can't get mad when I tell you what I think. I'm not Ms. Carter; I ain't gonna sugar coat shit for you, ok?"

"Okay girl, I can respect that." *He said, just as gay as he wanted to be before he continued.* *"Well, MJ has been trying to get at me for a while now. You know,*

sneaking little touches and feels here and there but I'm not really digging him. I've told him that I don't have those types of feelings for him but the man can be so persistent and sometimes I get lonely. A girl has needs you know." Damn, I thought to myself. Did this fool really think he was a woman?

"Okay, so what do you want my advice on?" I was trying to hurry up and get out of this awkward situation.

"Well, two days ago I made a huge mistake. I was feeling really lonely and Dom had yelled at me earlier in the day for some stupid shit I forgot to do. So anyway, MJ comes over to me and tells me he has some really important shit to show me, but it had to be in private. So I'm like ok cool, no problem. I follow him back up to his cell, cause you know everyone else was still downstairs in the rec room? Anyway, we get

back to his cell and he kisses me. I was like damn, what do I do? I told him ' You can't being doing that, you know I love Dom' and he's like, 'Dom don't go for that homo shit, so good luck with that, bitch'. "

As I sat there listening to his story, I began to find myself curious about whether or not Dom was a fruit tart as well. I had no idea that Tyson was gay let alone MJ. They didn't show any signs and they didn't have any tendencies. These boys are good at hiding that shit.

To sum up Tyson's story; he and MJ had some nasty gay sex, Tyson regretted it and told MJ he was going to profess his love to Dom, but when he went to do that Dom would barely listened to him and only wanted to talk about me. Of all the people he could have chosen to talk about, he wanted to talk about me. So now Tyson was tasked with getting information regarding my stats by a man he was secretly in love with.

Definitely some talk show shit.

July 27, 2000

While escorting Domingo to see the warden, I recalled the conversation I had had with Tyson one week earlier. I wondered if he and MJ were still 'doing the butt'. As I laughed to myself I heard a voice.

"What's so funny?" Domingo asked me. I hadn't realized that I had laughed out loud. Now he was starting intensely at me, waiting for a response.

"Nothing, just keep walking." I did not want him to know that Tyson had asked me questions regarding my status and informed me that he had a thing for me. I also did not want to get involved with any

undercover brothers. I don't go for that 'gay shit' as MJ would put it.

Domingo was 6'3, 205lbs, caramel complexion, smooth deep voice and a charm that worked on everyone, even the male CO's. He had a way about him that made him seem like a law abiding citizen. He related to everyone well.

"Did Tyson deliver the message? He told me he did. What did he tell you?" He asked with a bright, almost innocent smile.

"Do you believe your man? Maybe he isn't as reliable as you think he is. Maybe he has other intentions." I retorted with a sly grin.

"Oh he delivered the message. I know he did. That little faggot has a thing for me, but he thinks I don't know." I was shocked that he knew about Tyson feelings for him, yet he hadn't done anything and he saw shock plastered all over my face.

"No worries though, pretty lady. I specifically made him handle this task, so he would know that I was into women and not that homo shit. I love the ladies; I ain't into that gay shit, man. That's nasty, especially when there are women that look like you walking around." He said as he winked.

We reached the warden's office where they would discuss Domingo's upcoming parole board hearing among other things. I waited outside the door trying to listen in on the conversation. I wasn't able to pick up much more than the fact that the hearing would be in a few months and that the warden was rooting for Domingo to get out.

Apparently, the warden and Domingo's father had grown up together and were still fairly close.

Over the next few weeks, I had become somewhat of a personal chaperone.

I was always assigned to escort Domingo to his meetings with the warden, counseling sessions, the library...anywhere he had to go that required an escort, I was it. I have a strong feeling that the warden had something to do with it.

September 5, 2000

As usual, I was escorting Dom to the library. It seemed as if he purposely requested a library visit when no groups were headed over there.

He and I have become quite friendly. We have a few things in common like our sense of humor. He often asks me to tell the story Tyson told me about his relationship issues, just so he can laugh. We like the same kind of music, movies and books.

Needless to say, we have become quite fond of each other over the past months. Some days, he gives me a letter and tells me not to read it until I get home. I so willing obey and find myself filled with school-girl anticipation and excitement as I read his letters.

November 3, 2000

I was laying in bed reading Dom's most recent letter to me. He talked about how he planned to put the degree he earned before getting locked up, to good use. He talked about his future and how when he pictured it, I was always there even when he tried to imagine it without me. He talked about the feelings he had developed for me over the past eight months.

I had to admit, I was falling for him. I liked the deep conversations and the silly conversations we had. I liked the way he listened to me and made me feel important.

Just as I finished writing a response to him, my phone rang. The caller ID said New York State Penitentiary. I could not imagine who could be calling. I wasn't scheduled to work until tomorrow night; I hoped they weren't calling to ask me to come in.

"Hello." I answered hesitantly.

"Hello, may I speak with Andrea please?" The voice sounded too familiar, it couldn't be.

"This is she, may I ask who is calling?"

"It's Dom, baby girl. How are you doing?" He asked in a mellow tone as if telephone conversations between us were a regular occurrence.

"Dom? How did you get my number? How are you even calling? Where are you

calling from?" I was uneasy and it showed in my voice.

"Damn baby, you don't sound happy to hear from me."

"I am, but I just don't understand how you are pulling this off."

"Well, I ran into a little situation with Marquis and because I don't want anything to interfere with my board hearing I requested an emergency meeting with the warden."

"You're calling from the warden's office? Does he know? And what type of situation are you talking about?"

"Don't worry about all the details, baby. Let's just say that Mr. Johnson and I are no longer acquainted. And as far as the warden, he's sitting right here. I just told him I needed to hear my woman's voice before the hearing tomorrow, since I know you won't be here before it starts."

I couldn't believe that the warden allowed Dom to make a personal phone call from his office. I was now beginning to wonder if my job was in jeopardy.

"He knows you're calling me? He has to know. I can't believe this."

"Don't worry baby. He's not tripping about us. Plus I'm gonna be a free man very soon."

November 4, 2000

I arrived at work 15 minutes before my shift started, just to see if I could hear anything about the parole hearings held earlier in the day. I didn't want to seem overly interested in any one particular person so, I asked about everyone.

At 11:30 I was summoned to the warden's office. My stomach started to tie knots on top of knots. My palms became damp with the idea that my career was about to come to an end.

I walked into his office nervous and paranoid.

"Relax," he said "Dom told me about the two of you the first day you escorted him down here." You can't be serious I thought to myself.

"Sir, I am so" I began, but he put a hand up instructing me to stop.

"Domingo is just like his father. He came in here telling me how much he was interested in you and how much he wished he had a chance to get to know you, because he was so sure you were the one and blah, blah, blah. He was like a horse with blinders on, there was no convincing him otherwise. His mind was made up and I figured if you were willing to give him a chance knowing

the circumstances, maybe you were the one."

I left the office confident that the warden was on our side and hoped we really did have the strength to work out as a real couple when he was released. Speaking of which, I was also informed that he would be released on December 23rd. That was the best Christmas present I could have ever hoped for.

March 3, 2001

I got home from work at around 8:30. There was breakfast on the table, with my robe and slippers nearby. Dom did this almost every morning. He was the sweetest man I had ever met.

After his release in December, he went and stayed with some family for a while before moving in but even when he was with his family, we saw each other almost every other day. Then on New Year's Eve he proposed to me and I said yes.

We had still not made love, but we had come very close to it on several occasions. I told him the time we knew each other when he was still locked up did not count. He was disappointed like any normal man would be, but I told him I needed to know that he wanted to be with me and not my pussy. I needed to know that he felt I was worth it and that meant he couldn't go get his satisfaction from anyone else either.

I figured that if he was willing to wait, I was willing to work on our relationship. He waited, never giving me any indication that he had strayed nor did he ever pressure me.

"Dom, are you home?" I yelled out trying to figure out if he had already left for the day.

There was no response and though disappointed, this gave me some time to unwind and get some rest. I had the next two days off and planned to make good use of them.

I went into the bathroom where I found the tub filled with steaming water and candles surrounding it. He left me a note that said:

'Hey baby, I know you had a long day at work so I decided to do something nice for you. Enjoy your bath and your breakfast. I'll be back by the time you wake up from the nap I know you're going to take. ☺'

He knew me too well, I thought to myself. I was definitely going to take a nap after I ate and had my bath.

I woke up feeling refreshed but slightly confused. It was pitch black. I looked over at the clock and it read 8:30 p.m. Damn, had I really slept that long and didn't he say he'd be back? Where is he?

I walked into the living room and to my surprise; he had decorated it with a banner that said HAPPY BIRTHDAY! I was shocked. I had almost forgotten my own birthday. There were candles and incense burning. Dinner was on the table along with champagne. There were pink and red roses all over the room.

"Dom, you did all this?" I asked with tears in my eyes.

"Today is not only your birthday, but also one of our anniversaries." He must have seen the puzzled look on my face. "Today is one year to the day that we first met."

"Damn, it was my birthday when I did your intake. Wow, I didn't realize that."

"Well, happy birthday and happy anniversary baby!" He walked over to me and gave me a great big hug and scooped me up into his arms. He carried me to the table where he sat me down. He kissed me gently, and then walked to the other side.

We ate dinner and reminisced about the past year and everything that had happened. I didn't want to go out after dinner so we decided to stay in and watch movies.

I headed to the bathroom to take a quick shower to freshen up. I hadn't done anything all day but still felt the need to at least smell good for the man.

"How much longer will you be, sweetie?" Dom asked from behind the curtain.

"I'm almost done. What's that clicking noise I hear?" He was lighting more candles. He turned off the light and slipped into the shower with me. I tensed up.

"We don't have to go there if you don't want to; I just want to be close to you." He said as he kissed me.

I was nervous at first because I had never allowed him to see me completely naked, but all that anxiety was washed down the drain when he touched me.

He pressed his lean, toned bodied up against mine as I leaned against the wall and the water ran over us. He caressed my thighs as he kissed me and made sure I couldn't run away.

I found myself letting go of my inhibitions as he placed his manhood between my legs. It was warmer than the water and harder than he's ever been. He kissed my neck and sucked my nipples while his fingers played between my thighs.

"Damn, I love you woman." He whispered.

"You say that as if you don't want to." I whispered back before kissing him deeply again.

I kissed his neck, his chest, his belly button. I kept going and felt the surprise in his body when I put his tool in my mouth. I licked it and sucked it until he came.

He turned off the water and picked me up. With my legs wrapped around his waist he carried me into the bedroom. Gently he placed me on the bed.

"I want to make you feel good, baby." He said as he kissed the lips between my legs.

His tongue was hot and wet and juicy, just like my pussy. My body was on fire, yearning for him to be inside me. My body shivered and my mind whirled. He took me in as if I was the best thing he had ever tasted. He played with my nipples and my body couldn't take it anymore.

He positioned himself to enter into my yearning sanctuary, and stared into my eyes. I was more than ready to let him have his way with me. I've waited a year for this dick and I want that thug loving I know he's more than capable of.

"Dom… I want you to fuck me, we can make love later." I said as I stared back into his eyes. I did love this man, but there were so many nights when he was still incarcerated that I longed for him to ravage my body.

He looked at me for a second or two checking to see if I was thinking clearly, then he rose up, quickly flipped me onto my stomach and entered me from behind.

"I'm gonna fuck your brains out girl, you don't know what you're asking for." He said almost in a growl.

He grabbed my hair with his left hand, just enough to make me gasp, but not enough to hurt. 'Oh shit' I thought to myself, what the hell have I gotten myself into? This man is about to fuck me till it hurts.

He began to stroke, slow hard strokes at first, then long rapid strokes with my hair still in his hand. He slapped my ass and said, "This is my pussy. I'm gonna make this pussy beg for mercy."

He was handling his business and I could no longer hold in my exclamations.

"Holy Shit, Dom. You better beat this pussy up. Act like this pussy belongs to you!" I couldn't believe I had just said those things, but it turned him on because he started going even harder.

He took his right hand, placed it under by stomach a lifted me onto all fours. He let go of my hair and directed my hands to the headboard for support. He grabbed my waist and began to thrust himself in and out of me. In and out, in and out he went. I banged on the walls and screamed his name.

"Whose pussy is this?" He asked in that same low growl as he grabbed one of my breasts and continued to stroke.

He was on a mission with something to prove. The man was trying to kill me with his dick and it blew my mind.

"It's yours baby, it's yours!" I exclaimed as we both climaxed.

Well fell asleep with our bodies intertwined, but woke again 2 hours later for another round.

He ran his fingers up and down my spine as I lay with my body thrown across his. I lifted my head and kissed him passionately with all that I had.

"I love you, Dom." I said sincerely.

"Girl, you just love my doggy style." He said and we laughed together like we always had.

I climbed on top of him and straddle him.

"I do like your doggy style, but I might be able to impression with the way I ride." He licked his lips and caressed my breasts.

"I hear you talking..."
I got on that dick and tried to ride the living day lights out of it. I rode that thing like it was a mechanical bull and falling off was not an option.

This round was mine for the taking. I was in control and he was screaming my name.

"Damn 'Drea, are you trying to kill me? I can't, I can't take it."
He tried to make me slow down my stroke a few times, but to no avail. I handled my business and made his knees weak.

"Whose dick is this?" I asked in a dominating tone.
"Shit girl, it's yours. All day, baby. All day." I came first, and then he did.

Round two completed and we were both beat. We felt like we had just gone 12 rounds with Mike Tyson.

We lay in bed holding each other exchanging soft kisses and caresses. Suddenly, we heard someone beating on the door. We both looked at each other then at the clock. It was 4 a.m. who the hell could it be. The person banged on the door even harder.

I grabbed my robe and walked toward the door, with Dom following closely behind. I opened the door to see Tyson standing there pointing a gun in my face.

I had heard earlier in the week that he had been paroled for good behavior, but shit. We were both shocked to see him.

"What are you doing here?" Dom asked as he stepped in front of me, pushing me to the side.

"Oh don't act like you didn't know that I was in love with you, Domingo Justice." Tyson's voice was uneasy and filled with emotion. He stepped inside my living room waving the gun around as he spoke.

"I tried to tell you, but all you wanted to talk about was that bitch!" he yelled as he pointed the gun back at me. Domingo once again, pushed me to the side and stepped in front of the gun.

"What do you want from us Tyson?"
Dom sounded calm and in control.

"I just wanted you to love me back,
but NO you had to go and fuck around with
this bitch. What does she have that I don't?
A pussy? A pussy!"

"Ty, put the gun down so we can talk.
Why don't you sit down?" Dom was trying
to distract Ty. I looked on unsure of what to
do or say.

"Tyson, I'm sorry if I caused you any
pain..." I said trying to help the situation.

"Bitch! Don't say shit to me. You
knew. I told you!" He cried as the gun
waved back and forth.

Seeing that Tyson was focused on me,
Dom went for the gun. They fell to the floor
wrestling over it and I heard it go off four
times.

"Baby, I hear cop cars." I said to Dom as he held me in his arms.

"Yes, they're coming for us baby don't worry." He said to me with tears rolling down his cheeks.

"My stomach is burning. It really, really burns." I replied as I raised my hand up to see it covered in my own blood. "Oh shit." I said as I realized I had been shot.

"Don't worry baby you're gonna be just fine. That little faggot is dead and he won't be fucking up anyone else's lives."

"Baby, I just want you to know that I love you very much. I hope that you find someone who will make you as happy as you have made me." I began to cry.

"I won't be needing to find anyone, I've got who I need right here. Quit talking like you're trying to leave me. You can't leave me... I can't make it without you."

June 18, 2004

Dom and I have been married for two years now and we are happy. So many people were rooting against us and still are, but we're still standing.

"Dom, remember that you're supposed to meet me at the doctor's office at 2:30, okay?"

"Okay sweetie, I cancelled my meetings for this afternoon so I will be there on the dot. Love you, talk you later."

I got off the phone and went back to work. Since the incident, I quit working at the prison and began counseling delinquent teenagers at a special high school tailored just for inner city youth with behavioral problems. Dom kept his word and put that business degree to good use. He now works as an executive at a Manhattan based

~ 179 ~

brokerage company…imagine that. I guess the warden was really rooting for us. It just so happened that his wife was good friends with the owner of the company.

This was our third trip to the fertility clinic. We had decided we wanted children and we weren't getting any younger, but we ran into some road blocks.

"Please have a seat Mr. and Mrs. Justice." The doctor said as he gestured toward a couch.

"So Doc, what's the word?" Dom asked, anxious to hear something positive.

"Well, I'm afraid I have some bad news." I grabbed Dom's hand and waited for the bad news, scared of what it might be.

"Well, it seems that after doing some test, that the scar tissue that remained after the shooting is causing an obstruction in you

uterus. This is why the eggs won't stay put, so to speak, once they have been fertilized."

"So, are you saying that we'll never be able to have a child?" I asked as the tears began to flow.

"I'm not quite saying that, but I would recommend looking into surrogates or adoption."

Dom and I will not be able to have a child of our own because of some crazed obsession Tyson Dubois had for him. It's just unfortunate that he is not around to see and be punished for the effects his actions have had on our lives.

Though we may not be able to have children of our own, Dom and I still and will always have each other.

www.ingramcontent.com/pod-product-compliance
Lightning Source LLC
La Vergne TN
LVHW011350080426
835511LV00005B/231